NOBODY'S PERFECT!

NOBODY'S PERFECT!

✦

A CRITIQUE OF MODERN AMERICAN SOCIETY

Richard W. Glukstad

iUniverse, Inc.
New York Lincoln Shanghai

NOBODY'S PERFECT!
A CRITIQUE OF MODERN AMERICAN SOCIETY

iUniverse books may be ordered through booksellers or by contacting:

iUniverse
2021 Pine Lake Road, Suite 100
Lincoln, NE 68512
www.iuniverse.com
1-800-Authors (1-800-288-4677)

ISBN-13: 978-0-595-42084-1 (pbk)
ISBN-13: 978-0-595-86431-7 (ebk)
ISBN-10: 0-595-42084-2 (pbk)
ISBN-10: 0-595-86431-7 (ebk)

Printed in the United States of America

Contents

INTRODUCTION

We cut to the closing scene of the great movie *Some Like It Hot*. Tony Curtis, who is dressed in drag, is romantically being courted by Joe E. Brown in a rapidly speeding motor boat. Tony turns to Joe and whispers the truth about his true sexual identity, awaiting a possibly explosive reaction. But to his surprise, Joe simply answers "Nobody's perfect!

With this simple philosophy of life in mind, I propose to offer what I consider a long overdue analysis of the U.S.A. It is a kind of critique which tries to look at my nation as objectively as I humanly can.

I hear that America is the *greatest nation* on the face of the Earth. It may be the greatest, but it's not perfect, by any stretch of the imagination. My premise is that we are a nation of subconscious *seekers of perfection*. We are on a quest for the Impossible Dream while searching for The Holy Grail simultaneously. That kind of pressure is enough to turn anyone into a burned-out, drug-seeking nation of cranky people. (Does this sound like anyone you know?)

Let's look at the Webster's definition of the word *perfect* to see how close to the mark I am on this point of controversy. Remember, we are using the English language here, so we must think in terms of culture associated with the English-speaking peoples around the world. I stress this point because different languages produce distinct cultural variations of attitude and behavior that are inherent in everyday activity.

Perfect is an adjective, a kind of word that describes or modifies a noun; person, place, or thing. Enough grammar for today. Webster's first definition states that perfect means; <u>conforming absolutely to the</u> <u>description or definition of an</u> <u>ideal type</u>. It goes on to state that perfect also can mean; <u>excellent or complete</u> <u>beyond practical or theoretical</u> <u>improvement</u>.

If you examine these two definitions, some bells should go off in your head. The first bell should ring on the words *conforming absolutely* and then again on the word *ideal*. Again, bells should go off on the words *beyond improvement*. Webster's goes on to state that: Perfect describes an absolute, yes-or-no condition that cannot logically be said to exist in varying degrees. This statement brings to mind the Love It or Leave It mentality we have allowed our culture to develop and, at times, even encourage. To explain more, we need to illogically equate some ideas. First, we are the greatest nation on the face of the Earth (in essence perfect). Then the yes-or-no question enters, so we either love it or we have to leave it. Do we have no room for practical improvement? Have we also reached the ideal state of existence as a nation and people?

The English language, according to Webster's, states it has never agreed to this limitation on perfect's absolute yes-or-no condition. Perfect is compared in most of its general senses in all varieties of speech and writing. This really means that English speakers see perfect as a gray area that can't ever really be sighted or perhaps even attained on a personal level. So, this could mean that perfect can always be improved upon, like our *new and improved* American products. We know that only God is perfect, yet we keep striving to find it some place on Earth anyway, regardless of its cost to our peace of mind or physical condition.

Webster's also give a great example of this when it states; After all, one of the objectives of the writers of the U.S. Constitution was "to form a more perfect union." Need I say more about our use of the word perfect? We were born into this world as a nation to become more perfect. That is a very tough goal to achieve and I say it takes a hell of a lot of honing; so much, as a matter of fact, that by the time the honing is done, there is nothing left for us to use. Try sharpening a pencil too much, and see what happens to the perfect point you try to obtain; it breaks and falls off.

Are we, in essence, as Americans, like the useless pencil point, broken and off the edge? Not yet anyway, I can safely say. We are headed in that direction if we don't take stock of ourselves quickly. We need to keep on doing what is good with America, the things that as we say make it the greatest country in the world. Also, many issues that are retarding our progress, even crippling us as a leader of nations, must be addressed and rectified before that point falls off the pencil.

I am proud to be an American and when I travel abroad, feel a deep sense of pride and responsibility as a representative of the powerhouse of nations. Other peoples look at us as a marvel, a dynamo of energy and action. We are seen as take charge kind of guys with obstacles not an option. However, when I look introspectively at our *Gringo Nation*, I can't kid myself into thinking that everything is totally *kosher* at home. So let's sit down, take a deep breath, and take a hard look at the good, the bad, and the ugly of the U.S.A.... Let's try to make it that *more perfect union* that our Constitution demands of us all. Since nobody's perfect, I think there is plenty of room for improvement, as well as deep understanding and appreciation for the great things we already have and need to keep.

WHAT IS GOOD ABOUT AMERICA

THE U.S. CONSTITUTION:

To begin, let's talk about the **Federal Constitution** which finally began to work in the year 1783. It was a hodgepodge of compromises between small and large states. It was made as a trade off between the states rights ideals of Thomas Jefferson and the elitist-republican ideals of Alexander Hamilton. Small states like Rhode Island were afraid of being crushed by powerful large states such as New York. Nobody actually liked being told how to live, because each group of citizens, farmers, or merchants thought that their way of life was best. A better way could be to say that each one thought their life was just *perfect* for them.

Nobody wanted to give up what meant most to them, so what rights were not enumerated in the Federal Constitution were allowed to remain with the states. This way, everybody was happy and felt protected. However, nobody could foresee that these personal pleasures would someday overlap; making a lot of conflict for the people they were designed to protect and keep content. Things that didn't exist in the 1780's could have never been foreseen to get in the way of our *perfect union.*

An example of this *overlapping* I would like to use, concerns my present living arrangements in Miami, Florida. My family and I live in a large condominium complex on the fringes of the wetlands and near the Everglades. We not only must get along with our condo neighbors and its many by-laws, but our rock quarry miners to the west as well. It's an example of the big vs. the little guy, the organized vs. the disorganized. The problem lies in the fact that when my miner friends to the west blast out the rocks, the ensuing vibrations caused by the dynamite simply crack my floor tiles, vibrate the building, and crack the wall structure.

They never asked me or my neighbors if they could blast, as that right came from the State of Florida. To prove damage compensation, it is virtually impossible for me to do so. I need the pit number, time, and other proof to get any com-

1

pensation. The miners are so protected due to the money they generate to the state and its many politicos, that I don't stand a chance against them. But this is the tradeoff we make in a free society, where everybody is protected by the Constitution (some more than others.). The blasting is done in the afternoon when I am at work, so how could I ever pinpoint the time, as well as the rock pit, too?

In essence, we can see that our **Constitution** allows for the natural order of things to remain constant, in how the people with the most clout somehow outmatch those with less. But it doesn't completely allow for the devouring of the weak by the strong either. This is the beauty of it all in the end. If we were just fish in the ocean, we'd have the big ones eating the small ones everyday.

From the standpoint of philosophies, what we have created in America is a kind of protection of the weak from the strong. In my estimation, this is a result of the Republican-style elitism knowing where to draw the lines, as was done in ancient Greece or Rome in their paternalistic patronage of the lower class citizens of the Empires. Everybody had a place and a job to do in support of the Empire or Emperor. However, if a more Jeffersonian states' rights approach were in full control, then it probably would be a lot easier to bypass individual protections and steam roll right over the little guy.

One must not forget that our U.S. Constitution was created by a group of white men of British descent. Not only were they of one ethnic group from Europe, but most of them were landed gentry, highly educated gentleman farmers, and slave-holders as well, in many instances. My personal favorite, though we never had the pleasure to have met, was Thomas Jefferson. He wrote our Declaration of Independence, was considered a genius, and became the third President of the U.S. He fit into the landed gentry's category and did own slaves. Jefferson was the champion of states' rights in America because he was skeptical of outside governmental influences meddling in his local affairs. A Federal Government to him was like having a mother-in-law in the house. It's O.K. if she helps with the dishes, but watch out for the associated advice that goes with it.

American Constitutional organization is based upon English common law and the Magna Charta of the 13th Century. Here, English noblemen (not peasants) demanded guarantees that the King would not usurp their powers or control of their group of obedient and dependent peasants who worked their lands. Our Constitution did the same by enumerating specific guarantees to our people in the form of freedoms or rights, as they are now called. Some of them are the freedom to practice one's religion, assembly, speech, and right to bear arms, to name a very few.

What happened here was a very good way to create social stability in America. Now, we would not have Christians vs. Jews is some sort of religious bloodbath, or see Catholics and Protestants at each other's throats, as was the case in Europe for so many years. Another benefit to our Constitution's workings was that our country was founded by Protestant Europeans, rather than Catholic ones. Believe it or not, this was a blessing in disguise. What I mean by that is the social and political stability a Protestant-run country inherently gives to its citizens.

Look at Europe and you can see that the most wealthy and stable countries there overall are all Protestant-run or dominated. Catholic countries stress family above all else, rather than the collective economic harmony found in Protestant ones. Catholic countries however, are more fun to live in and have a fuller and richer artistic development. So, by placing the Protestant yolk of capitalist progress upon us all, America has been able to make greater progress than most countries in a shorter period of time than other countries make in lifetimes of upheaval and strife.

Catholic philosophy stresses more collective sharing, while the Protestant more favors the rights of the individual and his land ownership. Protestant philosophical control is tightly intertwined in our everyday lives through the creation of the government given to us by the Federal Constitution. Don't forget that our founding forefathers were almost exclusively Protestants, rather than Catholics or Jews, and that even today, as this book is being written; only one assassinated President was even Catholic. Hopefully, we might see a Jewish President in my lifetime at least, but it might be a better idea to check the odds in Vegas first before we place any bets.

OUR HETEROGENEOUS POPULATION:

If we take a blender and mix some dark rum, lime juice, brown sugar, and ice at a high rate of speed, a frozen daiquiri is created. We Americans are like that tasty yet potent and satisfying drink. We are a combination and conglomeration of a mixing of races and nationalities, and guess what? It hasn't hurt us, either, as the daiquiri wouldn't. It is truly hard to find a nation on earth where there is so much of a mixture of bloods.

Our mixture, by the way, has also allowed a lot of highly intelligent people to have been created as a side benefit to our continued leadership and greatness. Most black Americans and white Americans are not really either just one color or the other that is underneath the skins they wear. We are actually a nation composed of Indian, European, African, Asian and Middle Eastern or Semitic origins. There are also Pacific Islanders and Eskimo peoples, just to name a few others.

Everybody is here for a reason and everyone belongs together, as we are all the sons and daughters of God. Our DNA is all connected and intertwined, so who are we kidding when somebody thinks someone else doesn't belong? This kind of thought could make the INS unnecessary tomorrow. In the end, we all have common bonds that bind us together. To go a little further, let me list some examples of our commonality.

1. American Indian/Eskimo/Pacific Islanders: This link shows how peoples of Mongolian ancestry crossed the Pacific via the Alaskan passageway or Pacific Island hopping, and spread out across the Americas to become our American Indians. Some Chinese were even Jewish at one time. These extraordinary peoples intermarried with whites and blacks to form even more of a human American cocktail. The Miccosukee Tribe of Florida is an example of this incredible process of blood mixtures.

2. Europeans: These people are a hodgepodge of various tribes from all over Europe caused by tribal and imperial conquests. Included here are also Jews, Arabs, and North Africans, to name just a few, who found themselves living and working all over Europe. There was so much mixing in Europe that it is really almost impossible to tell if someone is actually what they say they are today. Gypsies are said to be from India and are spread all over Europe.

3. African: People from the second-largest continent are so varied in their makeup that their influence on us makes it less obvious at times to determine. Human life started in Africa, so right off the bat we are all of African descent. Africans came to America bought as a commodity. They came to us already mixed with Spanish blood lines, and through the Sicilians, as well.

4. Oriental/Asian: This is a group of peoples from the world's largest continent in size and population. Our Indian peoples directly come from them. They have mixed with Americans of all colors, as well as Europeans. A new cocktail of humanity has even been called Eurasian due to such a proliferation of new people.

5. Middle Eastern (Semitic): There are only two groups of Semitic people, Arabs or Jews. The offspring of Abraham, fighting ever since Biblical times, came to America in the beginning of its colonization period. Either they arrived disguised as a Spaniard or Portuguese colonizer, or they came openly with Columbus from the beginning. Non-Christian peoples had to profess

their Christian faith, or they were not allowed in the New World. Just say you were Catholic, and entrance was allowed to what were called the Conversos or converted ones.

Of course, these are the main groups of people, kind of lumped together to make the process easier to see. Everybody had a different reason for coming to America. Some arrived as political or religious refugees. Others came for economic reasons, while many were forced to come here against their will in bondage. But, for whatever reason, we are here together. Americans have built an incredible array of people that nobody can outperform, if we set our minds to it. Our collective experiences, based upon suffering in most instances, have created a tough, smart, and resilient people that have somehow become the role model for the world to emulate.

GEOGRAPHIC-STRATEGIC LOCATION

I don't want anyone to think for a New York minute that I have made Americans out to be *Ubermenchen* or a super race of special people that can fly faster than a speeding bullet or are more powerful than a locomotive. But our excellent natural geographic location didn't hurt us, either. Our place in the temperate zone between the Atlantic and Pacific Oceans has allowed us to prosper, where others' poor location have caused them to fail economically and socially.

The United States of America also happens to lie right between Europe and Asia, a fact that often gets forgotten in its importance. We were actually discovered by mistake in 1492 when Columbus was looking for a shorter way to Asia in order to bypass the Middle East. Those land routes for trade to the East had been blocked to Europeans as retaliation by the Muslims for the European Crusades on their turf. By keeping Europeans out of the Muslim-controlled lands, the necessity to get to Asia allowed alternative methods to be explored.

Columbus believed the world to be round, rather than flat, as many did at that time. So a way around the Middle East land route could possibly be done by sea to India or China. When our man C.C. got to the Bahamas in 1492, he *knew* he was in India, because he had not realized the New World even existed! Wow! What a surprise when he and his cohorts in adventure finally figured it out. More trips ensued, and the greedy development was on for Europeans.

Greed was, in my historical estimation, the number one motivating factor for our ultimate creation as a nation and people. It gave everyone the chance to come here in a kind of free-for-all. Any reason you had basically qualified you to enter the New World, and some had to come when they had no intention to do so.

You could be a Mongolian on the trek for food over the ice floes of the Pacific Ocean. Maybe you were just some West African who was at the wrong place at the wrong time, when he was captured by some other African tribe to be sold to the European or Arab slave traders. Perhaps you were a Chinese coolie laborer or shanty Irish laborer who got a job building the railroad across America.

Remember, the state of Georgia began as a debtor's colony for white indentured slaves, working off their European imposed royal debts. Rednecks seem to have gotten started this way as their white-skinned necks out in the field got real red under the hot Georgia sun. Australians, take note here, as it seems you mates got started in a similar way, except with a smattering of convicts, too.

As well as a supreme geographic location, America also happens to abound with raw materials that never seemed enough for the greedy Europeans that we come from. This incredible situation created new markets and unheard-of business opportunities, such as in tobacco and potatoes. Both commodities came from America as native species and got Europeans wealthy beyond their wildest dreams. Gold and silver was everywhere in America, making it easy pickings for the Spanish colonizers. They preferred to keep to the land that offered treasures and stick the Portuguese, French, or English with lands limited in mineral wealth. Peru had the gold while big Brazil did not, for example. Remember folks, Portuguese is spoken in Brazil and Spanish is spoken in Peru.

Opportunities abound in America and always will, based upon our historical way of development, with greed as its basis. Am I saying that greed is good? In and of itself, greed is bad and quite evil, so that is why I am not writing this book for the sake of greed and the money trail. My intention is to truly improve ourselves. Remember that nobody is perfect! However, some kind of greed is necessary and even admirable when it can lead to the development of opportunities that help others to a better way of life, with a higher standard of living than before. I suppose if greed did not exist, we would still be living in caves somewhere on the planet.

America gave our people the freedom to experiment in social, as well as business, situations that weren't allowed or developed in other societies or cultures. The development of the blue jean, or Levis, is the best example I can use to verify my claim to our world uniqueness. Here we have a German-Jewish immigrant tailor in America. By chance, in 1849 the California gold rush began. That tailor saw the need for tough pants for the miners and wound up making the utilitarian cotton blue jean for them. The material was actually invented in India, but used by poor Europeans for years. Somehow, through such overwhelming acceptance and practicality, Americans have converted the blue jean into a world-class fashion statement and world wide business for everyone interested in its profit potentials.

Jazz music is another great example of something uniquely American with worldwide popularity and acclaim. Started by African-Americans in the Deep South, at times used for funeral music, it has been transformed into multicultural art form loved by all. It helped unfreeze the cold war between Russia and the USA when sold out Russian concerts of American musicians made the headlines of the 1950's and '60's. The Walls Came Tumbling Down; jazz/biblical songs said it all.

CREATION OF THE "TOUGH AMERICAN"

Americans have created a kind of new breed persona that can be identified by nations of the world quickly and easily. The male counterpart would most likely be somebody who looks like the Marlboro Man. He is dressed in blue denim from head to toe, wears a cowboy hat, and has a rugged, manly face and stance either on foot or atop his horse. The "Tough American", as I call him is no wimp, speaks his mind, and doesn't take any crap from anybody. He is the product of years of a rough frontier lifestyle, combined with the large city dweller's environment. He's got street smarts, as well as a cowboy toughness and spirit.

When we make our American movies, the world gets to see what we are supposed to be like. Sometimes it looks like there could be some exaggeration, but I feel most of our movies portray us in a positive and accurate light most of the time. We in fact are tough people and not afraid of a good fight when necessary. On the other hand, we are loners, too, who prefer to be left alone in a peaceful environment, minding our own business. But watch out if we are treaded upon! We can strike back like a snake to kill our enemies without warning. One of our first American flags had the words DON'T TREAD ON ME emblazoned upon it over 200 years ago. A snake's picture was drawn there to emphasize the point.

Our national anthem, The Star Spangled Banner, ends with the words, "Land of the free and the home of the brave". There is no doubt in my mind we are really like that in many ways. We strive for freedom in our daily lives by everything we do and say. Our culture and customs speak volumes about freedom and how important it really is to all Americans. We are also very brave people, as we come from ancestors who had the guts to come here and to flourish under all odds of failure and desperation. We have fought and died to protect our freedom, as well as the freedom of people from all over the world.

Many nations of the world have not forgotten how we have helped them. They have not forgotten our fairness and generosity with their people as well.

They know that having the Americans there is better than not having them there at all. When we do business, we go the extra mile to show our concern for our clients. As the conquerors of the frontier and wilderness, we know how hard it is to make a buck and we go the extra mile to help others when needed.

However, let's not forget how we accomplished these great feats of great American strength. First of all, the Native Indians helped us along the way. Thanksgiving Holiday is proof of this. The English settlers would have died, had the Indians not come to their rescue with fresh food, supplies, and the shared knowledge of survival they imparted. We also need to give praise to the Mexican Vaquero, or cowboy, in how they imparted their way of life to our English-speaking Gringo cowboys in the Southwest. The Vaquero was keeping horses in *Corrals* before the Gringo knew that the Spanish word even existed.

Let's have a great round of applause for the most under-appreciated group in American History: the African-American. Their great strength and fortitude, combined with their enormous capacity for faith and patience, made us the great nation we are today. These incredible people made a home for themselves, even when they were rejected, killed, excluded, put down, and completely neglected as a necessary part of our American society. If I were in their shoes, I know that I could never be as brave as they in my daily life, with its ups and downs. I don't think it would be very easy for me to be so unforgiving and positive. In the mining business, it would be said that whites got the gold and blacks got the shaft.

The peoples of the Orient, especially the Chinese immigrants, also need time to be recognized in relation to their attributes of determination and industriousness. Many of them had to come here as common laborers to do the back-breaking work needed for mining and railroads. Laying track across the frontier was no small task, but they managed to do it, and do it well. Next time you eat at a Chinese restaurant, you may see a closely-knit family working together to serve you, from soup to fortune cookie. By working well together, families from the Orient have made the great leap forward, from poor laborer to well-off American citizen. Their children lead the nation in many areas of scholarship today and score the highest on SAT and GRE exams in the country.

LIMITATIONS NOT AN OPTION:

When President John F. Kennedy challenged Americans to be first on the Moon, he probably knew that we could get there before anyone else, even though he never saw the day himself. He knew that Americans liked to be challenged and that we needed a good one in order to make us get the lead out. Americans may not be the least lazy of nationalities, but never underestimate our ability to instantly turn from couch potato into a hot flash of energy across the Universe once challenged. If we get pissed off enough to do something, nothing can stop us. Our motto is "Don't hold me back, because here I come now."

We don't want to be considered just Hound Dogs; we want to be a nation of class. We won't allow ourselves to sit around and cry like a nation of babies, but rather crave distinction. We take our challenges to heart, unable to part with the convergence of dreams and reality. Great dreams are what built the United States of America, and their fulfillment is what we live on a daily basis. Perhaps this is why our detractors and enemies find so much to envy us for. Later in this book, we shall see why we are possibly not treating ourselves as number one in our own country. We love ourselves very much as a nation; however, lately we are not treating ourselves very well in many aspects of daily life and love. If we are still number one, we must never forget to treat ourselves as we want others to treat us, and that means "Cheeseburger all the way, please!"

Americans are like the great cheeseburger we invented. We are a combination of tasty meat covered with delicious fresh vegetables, smothered in hot fried onions, and embraced by two soft buns. Once you get a mouthful of us, you'll never forget it as long as you live. We are also possibly the most trusting of nations in the world. We like to give everybody the chance to be trusted. That is why we let so many different kinds of people to live and work in our country every day. Because we are a great nation of immigrants we have an innate ability to trust others, giving them the benefit of the doubt. Our ability to trust is the first test given new immigrants who come to America. Sometimes, if you give a man enough rope, he'll hang himself.

Our trust is like a section of rope. If the immigrant is bad, he'll probably hang himself anyway. But if he turns out to be O.K., he'll succeed in becoming another great American. Americans are not fools, as many think. Our trust is given because we never forget where we came from. Somebody also gave us a break. We're just returning the favor to the next guy off the boat. We are also quite trustworthy as a nation. I think we have done a terrific job as the leader of the free world. So far, we haven't blown each other up yet. This phenomenon is in part due to American trustworthiness as the world trustee.

Americans have been given the greatest responsibility of all time. That is to lead the world out of its petty differences and squabbles, into a new world order of peace, brotherhood, and prosperity. We have been unable to accomplish this yet since the end of World War 2, not because of our lack of trying or hard work. We have lost many chances to make a better world due to the terribly corrupt and despotic leadership of many of the other countries' regimes. The old saying of leading a horse to water and not having him drink most assuredly applies in many instances. The greatest enemy of any nation is its own leadership. Local leaders, chieftains, or dictators have been the death knell of many nations' chances for true progress. I am not saying here that our shit doesn't stink or that we have *the perfect* society. But what I do mean is to state that compared to many places on Earth today, Americans are light years ahead of almost everyone else, politically, economically, and socially. Our leadership and success has been, and will continue to be, based upon our great ability to trust. We trust each other, Americans trust strangers, and most of all we Trust in God to lead us down the right road in our desire to form a *more perfect union*. I don't agree that the abundance of security measures in our country is a true indication that we really don't trust each other. After all, every place has thieves and sociopaths who ruin the good things for the honest, hardworking majority of our citizens. However, our core values remain faithful and true to honesty and trust of our fellow Americans.

If it were so bad here, then how would we function daily? Every second, somebody pays for something honestly without robbing the person getting the money. Most Americans abhor dishonesty, vice, and violence associated with certain classes of crimes. We are actually one of the most church-going nations on Earth, and much more so than the Europeans from whence we came. We do have our fair share of atheists and agnostics, but on the whole Americans are God-fearing individualists.

FAIRNESS & EQUALITY:

One thing you may notice about the United States is our sense of fairness and attempt at equality under the law. Next time you are standing in the 10 items or less line at the supermarket, you'll probably see what I mean. Once I saw two *ladies* duke it out over that very issue precisely. One of the ladies was over the limit of ten items. She was gingerly reprimanded by the lady standing in line behind her, because of her apparent lack of concern for not respecting the supermarket laws. All of a sudden, all hell broke loose, and the two female subjects, as they were later called by police, went at it like two wild cats on the rampage.

America is such a big and heterogeneous nation that it has needed to develop certain social safeguards in order to prevent total anarchy and chaos. Little examples of the 10 items or less line reflect back on our foundations laid down for us in the Constitution. Our social, and especially our religious differences, respected by laws, have led us to behave properly in other areas that go unheeded or are out of control in many other countries. People soon find out that they might get their ass kicked or even have to go to jail for crossing the invisible line of respect, originally drawn for us by the nations founders, with the issuance of the Constitution.

People may live in the United States for a long time and get away with all sorts of dirty tricks. Everyone is given the freedom to be judged innocent until proven guilty. People are always given the benefit of the doubt and trusted to do the right thing. The wheels of justice do turn very slowly here sometimes too slowly. That is why so many people are always trying to pull a fast one. Many foreigners come here and see us as easy pickings. But just because we give everybody a break or a chance to do well doesn't mean that at all.

Americans have a lot of patience for negative, anti-social behavior. We try to treat those people with special programs and even provide psychologists geared to sociopath behavior disorders. We are willing to wait our turn quietly in a very long line. We may even camp out overnight, just to be first in order to get some special tickets or crack at a big break in a Hollywood movie. Just don't try to butt the line or you will be in for a big shock. That mild-mannered, patient American standing in line might just knock your block off, with everyone else cheering him on.

In contrast with other countries, Americans are actually pretty calm, well-mannered, and civilized. I remember an episode involving a bus trip in South America. You'd figure that that must have been a very normal, sedate experience, but it wasn't. First of all, just trying to get a bus ticket was an adventure in and of itself. There were no clearly marked places to buy tickets. Once you pushed and shoved your way to the head of the line, if you could call it one, you had to figure out which bus was going where and at what time. Buses had no specific schedule, only some sort of a destination with various stops on the way. Buses were composed of two major lines and other smaller ones, all competing for whoever showed up for a trip. Usually, a bus just scooped up the passengers hanging around the passenger zone if they had tickets. If that particular bus arrived first, it could get any passengers waiting around for transportation.

Buses actually raced each other up and down the mountain slopes, because whoever got there first picked up all the passengers he could squeeze on board. This kind of pure, free-spirited, and unbridled competition was very dangerous. On the way to where we were going, we saw a bus full of passengers that had just gone off the mountain road and crashed at least a thousand feet below into a ravine. Smoke bellowed up, but we slowed down long enough to take a good look. Other rescue people were already on their way down to help in any way possible.. But at that time and place,.nothing much could be done.

Only God really knew the true mechanical condition of the bus I rode those days around the mountains of South America. But I guess I was lucky enough to survive and thank God, too numb to any dangers present to even worry about it. Sometimes living on a cloud can have its good points. Take my word for it; there are millions of Americans living on a cloud today, totally immune to their surroundings or concerned about anything except their own feelings and sensory experiences. I am sure we aren't the only people to live on clouds, but we just seem to make an art form out of it all together. We are seemingly impervious to outside negative influences that might tear us away from Monday Night Football. Just because nuclear war hangs over our heads daily, why should Americans worry about it? If you're going to go off the cliff, you'll go off the cliff; just like that bus did in South America. Otherwise, there's no time to even think about it. Perhaps Americans are really the masters of Positive Thinking, after all. Positive Thinking trains us to block out negative thoughts and build upon only positive things that help us to succeed where others fail. Maybe America is great because we do live on a kind of cloud, above the rest of humanity and their nasty negativity.

The United States is actually a nation of Fundamental Protestantism with other religious groups mixed in for good measure. The next largest group is the Roman Catholics. Here lies the big difference. Catholics have a much more rigid and visible Church Hierarchy, from Pope down to parishioner. This historically entrenched system, I feel, causes an unseen distinction in social classes, whereas the Protestant version of Christianity lessens the blow to American society a bit. Our markedly Protestant nation seems to allow for an egalitarian system that doesn't exist in anyplace in the world. Europe and Latin America, for example, are societies where peoples' social classes are very distinct and well-defined.

In the United States, it is not so hard to crawl out of one's social morass and leap up to a much higher social position. More opportunity exists here for anyone willing to strike out on his own and take some risks. Other countries basically let you get to a glass ceiling, but never eat the carrots dangling in plain view. Bill Gates of Microsoft, the richest man alive, started out of a garage with some friends in the USA, a feat next to impossible in Europe or Latin America, for example. Do you really believe that the House of Windsor is going to let some South London bloke take over control or get his hands on the Crown Jewels? The answer to that question is: I don't think so! Queen Elizabeth even has problems adjusting to the fact that her son Prince Charles has to replace her someday. Her grasp on power is like the grasp on power of landed gentry and other high-class families throughout the world today. Their motto is: "Touch it and you'll get your hand cut off." America the Beautiful really can be a beautiful place if you only play your cards right. As the song says, you got to know when to hold, when to fold, and when to run. Unfortunately, in many other countries everybody mostly folds or runs to the United States to get their chance at the really big pot.

Our Great Sense of Humor:

By nature, most Americans are a *flippant* people and this special quality helps us to have in what is; my opinion the best sense of humor overall. The British come in a close second in their less slapstick and drier humor. Americans have the best of both worlds in that we have managed to combine and perfect the combination of slapstick with dry, subtle humor. We are able to accomplish this because of our British roots and culture, mixed with international flavors of multiethnic mixing.

Don't forget, we have the distinct advantage of having the great humor of the Afro-Americans, the Latinos (especially Mexican), and the wonderful and time-less humor of the American Jews, who came from every corner on Earth. Examples of my personal favorites are Steve Martin, Redd Foxx, Paul Rodriguez, and Billy Crystal. They represent all the kinds of different ethnic humor Americans are lucky enough to be blessed with. Our society has a wider range of humor because we are more able to relate to and understand the cultural nuances that make things funny in the world's cultures. Just because somebody from Tibet may think something is funny, that doesn't mean that an Indian thinks about it in the same vain. But an American understands many kinds of jokes better, simply due to the exposure he has had to so many different kinds of people. He may even be able to laugh at some silly story told about a yak in the mountains in Tibet, even though he's never been there.

Maybe you've seen bumper stickers stating: "You wouldn't understand: it's a Black thing." We'll, guess what, my friend? I may understand that *thing* just perfectly and have experienced the same situation, only with a twist, depending upon my ethnicity. People who produce bumper stickers like that haven't taken the time to make much contact with too many other ethnic groups but their own. The bottom line is that the more we exchange cultural values and experiences, and the more we mix it up, the less we see the differences among us.

The word *flippant* first came to my attention when I began teaching in the public schools of Miami, Florida. An older woman, the head of the social studies department at some jr. high school, referred to me as flippant over a matter which escapes me now. That dry and humorless school matron made me feel bad, but at the same time reinforced my determination not to change my personality in order to suit her or the school system's rigid rules of entrenched bureaucracy.

Flippant is a word that teachers customarily use in their arsenal of hurtful vocabulary in order to better control students. That day in my life has never left my psyche. It set the groundwork for me to quit public school teaching entirely about eight years later. The experience was a great example of how young caring teachers get turned off completely to the whole teaching process. It's the sensitive gifted people that public schools really need, yet those are precisely the ones who fall through the cracks or by the wayside onto the heap of millions of burned-out teachers.

Flippant, according to Webster's Dictionary means the following: 1.) frivolously disrespectful, shallow, or lacking in seriousness; characterized by levity. Here the humor comes into play. The idea of levity causing disrespect and as well appearing shallow should not be synonymous. Every situation and institution has room for humor and levity, especially our public school systems. Without sounding flippant here, our Public Schools are about as serious as a contestant in a dwarf-throwing contest on the Howard Stern Show. Howard Stern, in my humble opinion is the King of Flippancy. He is the greatest example of what is so funny about America; that is, in his way of flippantly remarking on so many social and political situations. If that school matron thought that I was flippant, it was only because Howard Stern was unknown to her at the time (1980's). Howard, by the way is half Jewish and half Italian, and from New York. He had the adventure of a lifetime by attending Black public schools in his hometown. The combination of experiences and mix of ethnic groups, must qualify him for the very special abilities I have been trying to explain to my readers. He is an example of a real American, an American with a keen wit and great sense of humor. He is the kind of guy able to appreciate and understand those Black, Mexican, Jewish, Italian, etc. things everyone goes through everyday of their lives.

A flippant person may not appear to be too patriotic on the surface; however it is exactly this personality who is the most patriotic of all! He loves his country the most, hurts when he sees all the injustice, inequality, and corruption so rampant now all over the world. The humor, conveyed through flippancy allows one to more effectively deal with, and even cure all those social ills. My motto is: "If it hurts, then get it out of you system, before it kills you from inside." Some people even think that constant doses of humor and jokes can cure patients with cancer. They may just be right. After all, cancer is a disease nobody is really sure about in how some people get it, while others don't. Maybe by becoming more flippant, Americans can cure cancer once and for all. Americans have a lack of reverence for the establishment because everything and everyone is a possible target for humor attacks. In order to survive these funny attacks upon their persona, many

American politicians and leaders have had to wind up doing a parody on them, somewhere on late night television.

By the way, when was the last time you ever heard of a world-famous German comedian? Do you begin to get what I am saying here? Nobody is as comical and really, truly funny as we are. We can even make love funny when we try. Sex, in and of itself, is actually quite funny when you begin to think of it. After all, it's all about bodily exchange of fluids, etc., but Americans have made jokes, movies, and funny stories all about it for years.

Americans like to laugh off almost everything they do, especially when things get very stressful. Our lack of reverence, even for the most reverent of things, has tremendously aided us in our daily lives in the ability to just cope better than others. Many foreign employers don't like to hire us to work with their organizations, particularly for this reason. Our lack of reverence, flippancy, and unique sense of humor is quite easily able to upset the most staid of European apple carts. After all, who needs some wise cracking *colonial* aboard when a nice quiet English lad will do as well?

For those of you not in the know, the term *colonial* is still used to refer to Americans by their British counterparts. We are considered a bit rough around the edges by Europeans, and for this reason also not highly desired as their employees. In the Middle East, it is very common to see British people working for American companies, but almost impossible to see Americans employed by British companies paying the same wages for similar services.

It is also much easier for us to make friends with different people abroad, than it is for them to make friends with us. I have found that when I worked abroad, people of other nationalities were usually very envious and jealous of Americans, either due to their better salary, housing, benefits, or cooler more laid back attitude toward the job situation in general. Sometimes, they would try to befriend us to gain some sort of material advantage like a better vehicle or access to some American club, where the drinks and atmosphere was better than theirs. It's not nice to generalize about such matters, but sometimes I was welcomed and aided by people of other nationalities while abroad. It is not the rule, to say that only Americans will help you, as there are generous and friendly people in all groups willing to lend a hand.

I don't mean to belabor the fact that so many Jewish comedians from the U.S. are so great, but just ask the French whom they really liked the best from our comical group. The name Jerry Lewis will pop up immediately. Jerry Lewis was considered to be a genius by the French public in his heyday. Jerry was perhaps not as well so understood by his own, as by the French nation. Sometimes a man can be a prophet only outside of his own land. Jerry Lewis could be considered a prophet of comedy in France, but not in America.

Sometimes American actors and comedians would even get into trouble at home, later getting blacklisted only to move to other places. A good example of such a comic genius who experienced trouble here was the world famous Charlie Chaplin. Due to his social and political activities, he had to leave America to live in, Europe for most of his life. Only, many years later before he died was he certified as kosher by America's political, social, and artistic establishment.

AMERICAN MUSIC AND ART:

Our music and art culture has been a leader all over the world, almost since the inception of the silent movie in the United States. American movies, an art form in and of itself, have allowed us to spread our artistic and cultural ideas to every country on Earth. Today, in fact, young men are lining up at the barber shops of Kabul, in order to get a haircut like Leonardo De Caprio had in the movie Titanic. If this doesn't prove my point, then I guess nothing does.

There exist today Elvis Presley cultists and impersonators all over the world, even after his death in 1977. People are lonely without him and want all their dreams to come true someday. They see themselves, praying for a day when all their aspirations and hopes turn real. Are these people just fools or do they have some sort of magic key to social and economic happiness? Maybe their *American* ideas are keeping them away from the negative vibrations found in their own squalid and nasty homeland. Those movies and *Elvis* kind of things allow them to build their lives a bit easier by accenting the positive light in their lives, rather than the real crap experienced everyday.

One of our greatest exports to the world was Mr. Louis Armstrong (Sachmo). Due to the fact he was born in the South during segregation times, this African American from Louisiana had to make his way abroad in order to get his break He played in France in the 1930's where he was considered a musical great, not only for his jazz trumpet, but his special vocal renditions of popular songs of the time. Europe had to tell us that one of our own indeed had incredible talent.

Rhythm and Blues music, born in the blackness of the South, was another great export to the world. It really took off in places like Newcastle, England. British groups like Eric Burdon and the Animals led the way in the music's proliferation. Eric Burdon had very close personal relationships with black American musicians from the 1960's and onward. Jimmy Hendrix was an example of Eric's closeness to black prophetic genius. This wonderful friendship allowed our music to gain even more power, acceptance, and popularity the world over.

Newcastle is a North English blue collar industrial city. Their pain and toughness somehow found a common thread with the pain, suffering, and toughness of African Americans. When you walk in someone's moccasins, you can understand their lives, pain and all. Eric Burdon in turn, had an innate insight into the R and B music of the American South. To play this music well, a person can't fake it. You either can feel it or you can't. A person with real soul can be white, in my opinion. It's just the experiences that make you soulful.

Like Moses, a prophet must usually travel outside his own land to be recognized a prophet. Do you really think that if Albert Einstein had never left his small town home in Germany, that he would have ever been considered a genius? Just the fact he was a Jew in Germany, born in Nazi times must speak for itself. It's like Sachmo of Louisiana fame. Leave or stagnate, my brother! Albert, had he stayed home, would have wound up as either a lamp shade, or a bar of soap in some German's house of the 1940's. Thank God he had a place like the United States to come to, later helping us to develop our nation's nuclear program.

By the way, Nazi Germany almost got the nuclear bomb first. At the end of WW2, Russia was very smart when they realized that whoever had the most German scientists would win the next war; the Cold War. As a matter of fact, the Russians exploded the first hydrogen bomb in 1949, ahead of the Americans; of course, with the help of their beloved German scientists.

America has learned that the way we stay ahead of the rest of the world is to become the rest of the world. "We Are the World" is not just the title of a song from the 1980's. Americans are the children of everybody and anybody. From the black Oriental, to the German Jew, we are truly a microcosm of the Earth's population. By having become everyone, we understand everyone. We feel their feelings, understand their thought processes, and have compassion for their needs, both emotional and material. We have children of the rich and children of the poor. Sometime their paths cross in America and they may even wed, to later make a new and improved kind of American.

So many pathways cross in America, because our great society of egalitarian democracy allows and even encourages it. Remember, our goal was *to form a more perfect union*. Somehow, by the criss-cross of paths, we have somehow found a great way to just do that very thing. As a matter of fact, our path crossing has even taken us to foreign countries and enabled us to further mix the pot with new and improved versions of the perfect American.

For example, after WW2, our presence in occupied West Germany allowed us to do that very thing. American music, movies, and culture spread there like wildfire. Young Germans, eager to embrace new world freedoms, took to us like ticks on a dog. They sucked our cultural blood dry. Germans got into things like cowboys, Harleys, and R and B-based music. German women were even brave enough to get it on with Black G.I.'s. Of course, babies were produced as automatic American citizens. Wow Adolf! What are you going to do now? We now perhaps have the master race you were looking for, when last we left you to do your twisted work. I now present the new and improved African American-German. *Zeig Heil* must now be followed by Bro! Do Germans really make the best Americans? Imagine a rocket scientist with soul!

The military occupation of Germany even attracted the early Beatles to the red light districts of Hamburg, Germany. There they cut their teeth on German and English versions of American R and B, as well as rock music. The Germans couldn't get enough of it, and the Beatles were lucky to have a piece of the USA in Europe, where they could get their musical feet wet. The Beatles went the way of American musicians, in how they were obliged to work abroad in order to become recognized and successful at home in the U.K. When the Beatles landed in New York on a Pan Am flight, they had actually been in America before, but through their West German experience.

AMERICAN GENEROSITY:

Ask any taxi cab driver in the world who the best customers and tippers in the world are. I can guarantee you that they will unanimously say the Americans are champs. Our benevolence and generosity are a way in which we give a leg up to people when they come to live among us. Many immigrants begin their lives in the USA as cab drivers themselves, going on to bigger and better things later. Americans are not usually cheapskates, like so many other people from all over the world.

"Tip" is an acronym for the phrase, to insure promptness. When somebody busts their hump for you, does the best they can, and insures prompt service, he deserves a little something extra, in addition to the standard payment. Americans are appreciative of such efforts and reward people well for their efforts. Though this is the case in the USA, it is not like this in most of the rest of the world. A person can bust his ass and still get it kicked later, just because he didn't kiss somebody else's. Tipping is not a city in China, as one American comedian once said. Tipping shows others they care, appreciate, and want to help somebody that might not be as well off. Some people come to the United States with their air of superiority and try to pass it off here. But fortunately, some tough American usually puts them in their place quickly when they try to pull off one of their selfish stunts. Egocentric sociopaths abound here and abroad, but the USA is a Waterloo for many of them. We have a special kind of way to fry the big fish, along with the regular-sized ones.

Many people prefer not to socialize too much with Americans for this very reason. We have a thin skin for jerks and stupid asses of all nationalities. Our uncanny ability to spot one evokes fear in the hearts of foreigners. Our generosity helps us in the long run. The extra money we spread around so freely comes back to us in many ways, both seen and unseen. The actions give us a positive spin to the world and makes people want to be our ally. When somebody sees the sign Made in America, they immediately want to buy into it.

American generosity makes social and business common sense. It's just too bad that some other people in the world can't or don't want to understand it. Perhaps their limited world view is only concerned with their own *immediate* gratification. Gratification is never to be seen in terms of the here and now. Long-term strategies need to be given preference, because what you do today will come back to affect you in the future. Just remember that the toe you step on today could be connected to the foot that will kick you in the ass tomorrow. You could say that Americans know it is nice to be important, but that we have also learned along the way that it's more important to be nice! As long as we can remember where we come from, remain humble and generous as a nation, it will be very hard indeed for some other nation to knock us off our roost.

The demise of thinking, most prominently experienced in the industrialized and techno savvy West, has been the reason for the substitution of so many *procedures* we now find in American workplaces. Americans in and of themselves are really smart and nice people, but their lack of freedom to think and therefore perform spontaneously have hampered our ability to effectively perform as our individualistic ancestors did so well. Too many times, those *procedures* force outsiders to think of us as insensitive dumb robots. Sorry, we don't do that!" is the name of that game. Not everyone is able to buy into that take it-or-leave it style, so they just get turned off. You guessed it, they have become hard-core anti-American.

I am not looking for excuses why our shit stinks sometimes, but since nobody is perfect, even our occasional stink can be forgiven. After all, when a people live and work in a highly technologically advanced society and country, it's only normal for a certain level of robot-like behavior to rub off on them. This phenomenon seemed to have begun sometime after WW2, a war where radar, rockets, computer like gadgets, and atomic weapons were first used to kill people.

America conquered the Nazis, however the Nazi-like mentality of the Germans left to run Germany also rubbed of on us through a process of osmosis. Remember that birds of a feather flock together. So many years of contact with

Germans inside their lair has taken its social toll upon Americans. The Spanish author Ortega y Gasset in his book, <u>The Rebellion</u> of the Masses, talks about this post war robotic-like change of people in general. Americans may have become desensitized to the world around them, but unfortunately we are not alone. It's just that Americans stand out like a sore thumb from the rest of the world, no matter what the scenario. We get the bad press, while the rest of the world escapes criticism most of the time.

THE AMERICAN FREE-MARKET SYSTEM

Americans have enjoyed unparalleled economic strength and progress, due to their free market system, a system marked by the free flow and exchange of goods. Our mighty economic engine accounts for roughly 40% of the world's real output of goods and services. That means that the rest of the world combined puts out the other 60% of whatever is produced and/or used. For example, our State of California has an economy the size of the entire country of Brazil.

The United States has unlimited job opportunities because of this great free-market economy. It allows everyone the chance at being a homeowner, something unheard-of in so many other places on Earth. Remember that the real reason people are lining up to live in my land of the free and the home of the brave is because of the green color of my money. *"Show me the money!"* Is the world's cry. I don't see anybody trying to rip the doors off too many other places in order to get in with their in-crowd.

We also make it very easy to travel anywhere. Our roads, expressways, and modes of transportation allow a coast-to-coast trip really easy. If Americans want to travel abroad, our low-cost fares make it possible for us to do so. The fares are low-cost to us, because the green stuff we make is a *hard currency,* rather than some devalued banana republic peso. Our engine shits when we get on the pot. We don't just pass wind all day, hoping to make something come out. We actually make something of our time, because we truly understand the meaning of "time equals money". We build and save for the future and don't blow our wads every weekend, only to have to start over from scratch again.

Our currency is hard because we are a nation of serious and basically honest people. Our business and government are constantly intertwined in order to produce a place that means business, but not monkey business. When a Japanese or British investor places his trust in our country, he knows that his chances of losing the whole enchilada are a lot less remote than if he had invested in another country. The dollar is the world benchmark of economic investment and stability. Most everything in the world is priced in terms of US dollars. Other world currencies base their money upon the value of our money, because they know that we are stable enough as a nation to do so.

A corrupt nation of slackers will never be able to surpass the American economic power, which we have created from hard work, honesty, integrity, imagination, ingenuity, determination, cross-cultural interaction, toleration, freedom, and bravery. If I have left anything out, feel free to interject an adjective. At this juncture, I'm sure I open the floodgates to take on lots of negative criticism about my country, but that is fine, and we can take it in our stride. I know that not everybody loves us as much as I do, but that is to be expected when you are on top. There's always somebody out there trying to knock you off the top of the heap, in order to take your place. But as previously stated, we are the world, so how can we ever be knocked out by ourselves? We would have to commit social and economic suicide to do so, and I can't see it ever happening, at least in my lifetime.

Americans enjoy a very enviable standard of living, so why not kick back and enjoy the fruits of one's labor? That's exactly what we do, Charlie! Our leisure time activities are, bar none, the most varied and free spirited in the world. We have every sort of way to spend the day or night, in order to circulate the money to somebody else who needs some green stuff, too. When some Shriner comes to Miami Beach for his yearly international convention, the money flows like water, as happy working guys unwind and relax with their buddies. But remember, if they were *from hunger*, then that generous freedom to do so wouldn't be at all possible. If somebody can name a recreational activity that is not celebrated here, I'd like to know about is, just to begin it here myself. Sports abound in the USA, with our Olympic team being the world's largest. We may not be the best in every field of recreational sport, but at least we give it a shot.

Americans account for about 90% of the world cruise market today, with the Port of Miami being the world's largest. Honey, when you can afford to cruise, then you know you have done something right in your life. Just ask the cruise ship employee who treats them the best at the end of the cruise; that is when the little envelopes are handed out! It sure isn't anybody else other than those *Bloody Colonials*.

Target and skeet shooting, as well as hunting, are examples of popular American sports and leisure-time activities, not even allowed anymore in some parts of the world. We are still free enough to do so, thank God! But just ask somebody from the UK how they may think on the subject, and what you'll get is an illogical rationalization of how much safer they are, because their government is now making it almost impossible to do these things. All I know is that when a government sets up video cameras everywhere and at the same time takes guns out of their subjects' hands, it shows two things to the rest of the world. One, that it doesn't trust them, and two, it is either a police state now or will become one sometime very soon.

You should realize that people of the UK are not citizens, but subjects of the Queen. With a whim of the British Crown, one of its subjects can get the severest of treatment for having only offended them publicly. Americans are citizens of a full constitutional democracy, with every right to say what they want about its leaders, such as our President or Supreme Court Justices. Try poking fun at Saddam Hussein, King Abdullah, or the current President of North Korea, and see how far you get. Perhaps in Cuba, Fidel Castro would throw you in prison, or even worse, send you to Miami. However, Fidel would be doing them a great favor in allowing them to escape his totalitarian regime. Just remember the great motto of the police state: if you don't do anything wrong, you'll have nothing to fear. This way of thinking does not justify government mistrust and 24-hour surveillance of its citizenry. Who gets to decide what is right and what is wrong, anyway? It surely won't be some guy driving a truck for a living, that's for sure.

Another part of our country, which is severely taken for granted, is its public utilities: phone, electric, gas, water and sewer systems. Every time we turn on the light, flush the toilet, or go for the water faucet or cook, we live a very nice comfortable life. We have access to the best infrastructure of public utilities anywhere. Some people squat over a hole instead. Other non-Americans drink highly contaminated water or heat their food with kerosene, that is, if they can find it. Believe me when I tell you that I once had to use a very heavy political connection in order to get a phone line connected to my house in South America. Could anyone in the USA actually imagine having to call a senator to get a phone line in your home? I don't think so.

The reality remains that Americans are free to take for granted many daily things that others in the rest of the world only dream of. Another great service offered in the USA is its incredible emergency response network of 911 emergency fire rescue and paramedics. When you think you are having the big one, just call 911. Somebody will rush to your door in hopes of saving your precious life. They may give you CPR or even jolt your heart with electric current so you don't slip into the bonds of death.

Maybe the paramedics will have to take you to a hospital in one of their well-equipped ambulances. Chances are you'll not only survive the ride, but wind up getting some of the best medical treatment in the world to boot. We truly have a superior medical system. Many people apply for tourist visas just to jump in a taxi and head for an American hospital once they get to the airport in the USA. They know they will get excellent and probably free treatment.

Americans like to share what they have, even when they have very little. A noted American Archbishop likes to tell stories of his beloved grandmother, a humble seamstress. Even though his grandma had almost nothing herself, she could always find at least one dollar to send off to one foreign missionary or the other in real need, because those people she helped had much less than her. Difficult times are not an excuse for Americans to say "no" to the truly needy. We make sacrifices to help people who have very little all over the planet.

America's enemies are not even immune from our generosity, because we even help them as well. After WW2 ended, Americans sent monetary assistance to the families of German soldiers, whose sons recently fought against their American sons. We truly take the advice of Jesus Christ by turning the other cheek. We know well that by giving a helping hand to someone you just defeated, you will make a long-lasting friend, thereby making it much harder for him to try and hurt you once again.

The USA still allows a lot of immigration into its legal borders. World immigration never stops into the USA, and as a nation of immigrants we have never forgotten the words of the great Jewish-American poetess, Emma Lazarus; her words adorn the plaque at the Statue of Liberty in New York Harbor: "Give me your tired, your poor, your huddled masses yearning to be free!" I suppose that piece of American poetry sums it all up for us, and shall continue to do so forever.

Once an immigrant lives successfully here for at least five years, he can become an American citizen and be the proud owner of an American Passport. Let me tell you; the holder of an American Passport abroad is considered to be a very special thing. It opens doors much easier and wider than for those with different citizenships. Take my word for it sports fans, we are trusted, admired, and even revered by members of many nations just because we are Americans. It is almost as if we are a kind of rock star or other celebrity to others.

In the United States of America, we organize ourselves so well into groups that we cater to everyone's need and interests. Just look around, and you will see every possible need, organized into some sort of group, with its sole function of finding help and service to its members, as well as their community in general. When Americans form groups to help each other's particular need, they most likely also reach out to others not as well off as them once again, in order to find a way they can be of service to them. America is a land where real tough baby boomer bikers reach out to help fluffy little kids in distress.

Our social grouping also allows each American to help himself as well. The interaction of people gives us a great chance to meet new and interesting people with similar interests. We can meet others that can change and even enrich our lives, by helping us to find solutions to many of our personal problems. After all, isn't life all about trying to be the best you can? Isn't life about being happy, healthy, and wealthy? By and large, Americans are a nation of these sorts of people." I'll buy you a Cadillac" as the song says; keeps anyone pretty content. In the United States, you don't even have to be rich to buy one. A nice used Caddy in mint condition can be bought by virtually anybody with a steady job in the USA.

We can cruise up one of our fabulous free-interstate highways in our smooth running Caddy, filled with pretty cheap gas anytime we desire. Atlantic to Pacific coast trips are a breeze for us. As we drive, listening to satellite radio, with the GPS kicked in, Americans are on the path to freedom and happiness.

Some soldier fresh out of the Army can achieve his dream this way in only a flash. Here, a military veteran is helped by his country with all sorts of social and economic perks. We just don't give out a bunch of rusty medals and dusty ribbons to reward our boys. Veterans have their own government-led Administration to oversee their welfare. From the sick vet to the healthy Young Turk, we make sure they are not left to fend for themselves. Veterans organizations abound in America for that help they so deserve, in the defense of our freedoms. Veterans even have preference in job applications, especially in concern with civil service employment.

Now that booze is legal once again, as it wasn't in the era of Prohibition last century, an American can drink alcohol to his heart's delight. We have every flavor here under the sun, and beer festivals abound. We are assured of safe and delicious alcoholic beverages. They are all legalized and regulated with regard to their quality and sales. Minors are forbidden from consuming alcoholic drink. The various governmental agencies actually do a very good job enforcing the laws to protect youngsters from the possible adverse effects of drinking. Many countries do almost nothing in this area; kids are seen drinking there with almost no consequences.

By now, you are probably close to puking on yourself from having read such glowing and syrupy things about my fellow Americans. But, I don't think that anything I've stated is not really true. So far what I've done is to emphasize the good things about my country and stay away from the dark side, the negative, the bad and the ugly things haunting everybody alive today. Our problems as Americans are also the world's problems. We are nations, very intertwined on a big blue ball that is constantly traveling through space and always in flux.

The world has made America the great nation that it is today, and we owe it to the entire world, not just ourselves, to set the example to be the best we can; strive to make America a perfect union of a brotherhood and sisterhood of Americans and responsible world citizens, too. If we fail to stop trying to achieve our concept of a perfect union, we will be doomed to the dust heaps of forgotten and once-great nation-states, whose empires have been lost in the world's shuffle to get to the top of the heap. Remember, we may be on top of the heap today, but tomorrow may bring many surprises to America. If we are caught off guard by our Hubris, or false sense of pride, we shall fall hard. The bigger they are, the harder they fall prediction will come to pass once again. In the world scheme of things, it really won't make much difference anyway. But wouldn't it be a shame, that we knew how to stop it and chose not to do so?

As a great lover of the United States of America and proud American citizen, I deem it necessary and immediately essential to bring certain things to your attention, things which may not be popular or received well at all, but truly needed if we are to save America from its own demise. I just can't sit back in my easy chair, turn on the tube, stuff my face, and sleep well if I don't at least attempt to improve our quest for a more perfect union.

In my opinion, Americans are on the right road most of the time, but once in a while we may need a little guidance or shift of gears to get where we really want and need to go. Getting to that *more perfect union* isn't easy, but if we close our eyes and try to drive there that way, the trip is surely to end in failure and disaster. "Living is easy with eyes closed; its understanding all you see." is a rough road to take, according to the Beatles song, however the only alternative we have to being on "The Eve of Destruction".

Many of my personal ideas are rooted in great Judeo-Christian ethical and moral concepts that come straight out of the Old and New Testaments of the Holy Bible. People who don't try to understand what the Bible offers us in advice and wisdom really lack a great tool for daily life. The USA was founded by groups of seriously religious peoples, to a large extent. However, as the time passed, their ideas of religious toleration and conduct were conveniently cast aside to make way for a more modern form of Economic *Christianity* as I call it, for no better term to use. Orthodox Judaism was also greatly changed by the Reform Movement in America, to make it almost impossible to distinguish a Jew from his Christian countryman. I first was shocked and made aware of such behavior when I was invited to Shorty's Bar BQue in Miami by none other than a reform Rabbi and his entire immediate family. We were served heaping portions of everything non-Kosher, from pork, beef and chicken.

As a young boy, I felt strange eating in such a place with the Reform Rabbi and his family. The Rabbi appeared completely comfortable in his public display of non-Kosher food consumption. He didn't act ashamed, uncomfortable, or even guilty for his actions, because according to the Reform wing of Judaism, it's perfectly *kosher* to do so. However, this use of the word Kosher here is not really kosher. I am using it with my tongue in my cheek only to make a point. The point is that, as the Rabbi has distanced himself from his roots and foundations, so has his Christian brothers and sisters in America.

Because America is so rich and because time is money, many of our most important rituals and religious mores, as well as folkways have been sublimated to the all-mighty acquisition of the greenback. The society of the great consumer has shaved off its beard, shed the black hats and clothes to embrace a quick study in Madison Avenue lifestyles. Remember that the pagan Egyptians invented shaving and that our Holy Bible tells us not to eat and consume certain foods. So why do we do it anyway? The answer is that once the cultural distance is too great from the origins, it's usually too late to turn back the clock.

Of course, it's not impossible to revert to one's roots, but economically speaking, it is usually such a sacrifice to do so that nobody really wants to try it. If a man has to go to work clean-shaven on the Sabbath, the immediate problem of survival rears its ugly head. Should he shave and work, or tell the multinational company that he works for that his core religious beliefs come first? What do you do when you can't find kosher food in some town that you have to go to in order to do business for your employer? These kinds of problems can affect Christian women who refuse to wear pants to work when required. But since we have distanced ourselves from what is holy, America has settled for giving to God its leftovers. Let me tell you, God does not like to get anybody's leftovers. What God really wants is what is due, and that is <u>our best</u>. America needs to stop doling out its seconds and give to God what He is owed. In order to continue to get the blessings of God as a nation the USA needs to keep giving its best; keep trying to form that more perfect union, as our religious forefathers demanded from themselves over 200 years ago.

Have we strayed from the path set for us by America's founders? My answer is a resounding yes, however we have not gone too far away either. At least we still know where the path is located, and it's also in plain sight. We have the opportunity to fix and improve, as our nation is not broken beyond repair. But if Americans continue to be complacent by ignoring or just socially sublimating everything, we can not keep our nation alive. We will be *A Town without a Pity,* as Gene Pitney wrote in his smash hit. Those little minds shall tear us apart for-ever.

The alternative to not getting God's blessings is to incur God's wrath and be cursed! If we help God, then God will help us. But we need to make some sacri-fices, as God sacrificed his only begotten son for the sins of the world. Americans must be ready to recognize the Messiah when he returns once again. However, we can't see him unless we have the spirit as did Simeon, the Biblical prophet who recognized Jesus as the Messiah, while those around him failed to do so.

Our salvation as a nation rests in our response, or will we fail to see him? Without the *Spirit*, we have no chance. So let's try to get it real fast. God's actions were done for our benefit; we just need to give back to him what is due. The alternative for continued disobedience is failure and suffering. God has prepared us to offer sacrifice; we need only to receive Jesus to be prepared for everlasting life as a nation and as a *People of the Book.* All the good we have accomplished for ourselves and the world was based upon our religious foundations, not rules of *Economic Democracy* and expediency. Our *more perfect union* is currently off track, and we really need to get back on track before the train crashes or even reaches a station we don't ever want to go to anyway. Will we become just another banana republic to be forgotten on the dust heap of vanquished empires? I for one don't hope so, my fellow Americans. So lets see what we can do to change our destiny. Let's save America from its own internal demise and make peace with ourselves, instead of being our own worst enemy.

So, you may ask what's really wrong with the USA? I can tell you that there are so many things wrong with us that I had to write a book to enumerate them. Do you think it may be too late to go back and fix everything? I don't think so at all. We have immense recuperative powers and can regenerate ourselves as a star-fish grows a new arm. After all, since we are the world, we must have a few worldly tricks up our sleeves to get on with the business of improvement. The slogan "Don't fix it if it ain't broke." holds no water, as far as I am concerned.

When a nation is young and strong, full of energy and life, it doesn't heed much advice to reform itself. But we may be dead, as a nation, before our time is due. We have already hit the 200 mark and, in my opinion, made no significant change to ensure our continued survival. Our form of government still exists, yet is being circumvented as our religious lives and foundations are circumvented in the name of *progress*. Yet is it progress when we still have inequality, suffering, poverty, and a culture of death at home? If your refrigerator is empty, have you actually made any tangible progress, just because you have the refrigerator? Any sane person knows that the answer is no! Let's see what we can do now to smell our shit and if, necessary, analyze the cause of the stench we produce. Perhaps, someday American shit won't smell as badly as it does right now. Then and only then can we say to our world brothers that we really are the *Greatest Nation on the Earth*.

WHAT'S WRONG WITH AMERICA?

"Mankind are more disposed to suffer, while Evils are sufferable, than to right themselves by abolishing the Forms to which they are accustomed." (The Declaration of Independence) In Congress; July 4, 1776.

Sometimes a person's greatest strengths can also be the cause of his greatest weakness. In the case of the USA, our Constitution is our greatest strength, in how it has allowed for continued democracy and prosperity for such a long time. It's even the basis and model of many other countries' new adventures in democracy. However, the flip side and rough underbelly of our great government is a hodgepodge of contradictory state-to-state laws, rules, and regulations.

Yes, my fellow Americans, confusion has been created as a result of allowing every state to try to have its cake and eat it, too. The idea of States' Rights, though noble in nature over 200 years ago, was designed for only 13 former colonies, all of which had almost everything in common in the beginning of the existence of our nation.

Our founding forefathers were all white guys of English stock from a Protestant background. Many were landed gentry or wealthy businessmen, with higher levels of education than the masses they represented. They also had special interests which they demanded be defended in their home states, before they finally decided to form that more perfect union, and sign their names on the dotted lines of the Constitution.

On paper, this all sounded great and appeared to work well for a very long time, that is, until the inherent makeup of the USA changed, to the point where it is unrecognizable from its early origins. Now we have a lack of cohesion, socially, politically, and economically from one state to the other. The ensuing differences in turn have caused great disparity economically from state to state. It's no accident that the poorest major city in the USA lies in the South, in a state which is *Mickey Mouse* by nature. It's my birthplace; the City of Miami, Florida, now controlled by banana-Republicans. I am ashamed to say that in my State of

Florida, teachers are not allowed to strike at all. Imagine how their lack of such a great weapon diminishes their power at the bargaining table!

You see, the South is a *right-to-work* area of the country. A right-to-work state allows nonunion members to get all the bargained-for union benefits, without having to join the union. In essence, it is a legalized way to kill union membership and discourage union participation. The South at one time was a bastion of slavery and agriculture. Florida, for example, was like a great food bank for Rebel troops during the Civil War. As we see, not much has changed since slavery times in the Old South. Wages and workers rights remain at the bottom of the barrel, when stacked against people who work in the North. Wages for blue collar jobs are usually half in right to work areas, vs. places that have decent union organization and benefits.

The old philosophies of landed gentry and master-slave work relationships still prevail in many areas of the South, especially where they allow undocumented aliens from south of the border to work like the slaves they once owned. It's no accident that so many undocumented workers live around border towns or in Florida, with its miles of poorly guarded coastline.

When a Colombian enters the USA *por el hueco,* (through the hole), he really does go through a hole at times. That hole can be underneath a house on the border with Mexico. It can also mean all the holes in our National Parks, with international borders in Canada as well. Here, thousands of economic slaves are waltzed across the border by trained guides who know every trick in the book in order to get somebody inside *Gringolandia,* or the land of the Gringo.

When Boo-Boo asked Yogi if he saw anything funny, the Park Ranger was never around, was he? That's because Mr. Ranger was actually told to look the other way. Why? Well, that's because the Dept. of Interior, which governs National Parks, is not allowed to enforce Border Patrol or INS functions, from the Dept. of Justice. Hey! What government worker wants to work extra anyway? If somebody can officially get out of doing something extra, I think that should be reason enough. Remember, no government can ever replace private sector efficiency when asked to do so.

I can assure you that my condominium and all the other homes in my area of Miami-Dade County were built by nonunion Latinos, whose legal status is surely very hazy, to say the least. The only legal ones had to have been the Cuban builders, themselves; but they don't lay the bricks or dig trenches anymore. So, some guy from Mexico works like hell wound up making the walls where I live. He works like hell and for a lot less than a Gringo, in order to send home money to his struggling family. When things get better, the whole family is sent through *el hueco,* and meets up with him in Miami. The family usually rents a small run-down apartment in Little Havana or Allapattah, to settle down to the American Dream.

That American Dream can turn on a dime into a real nightmare for that immigrant family. That overcrowded apartment, full of an assortment of men, women, and children, takes its toll on everyone. The backbreaking construction work almost seven days per week does as well. The man who works like hell also begins to drink like hell in order to relax and numb his feelings of drudgery. He can come home one day and start taking it all out on his stressed-out wife. The kids are present when everything blows, and begin to scream and cry out for it to all stop.

It stops when the cops knock on the door and take somebody downtown for whatever legal infraction. But a few days later, a State Investigator also knocks on the same door, because the cops turn their report of domestic violence over to the Dept. of Children and Families. Domestic Violence in the presence of a child is also a crime, such a kind of crime that the child or children present can be taken away from their parents by the State.

Can you imagine what a feeling of overwhelming helplessness and confusion somebody who can't speak English might feel at that point? But ask yourself why it all happens anyway. First of all, the whole family shouldn't even be here in the first place, yet they are. They are here to feed the greed by cutting corners in the economic scheme of things. Remember that a guy who really isn't here can't bitch too much about his working conditions and social status.

I just had another brainstorm. If the cops intervened in the aforementioned social scandal, why didn't the whole family just get put on a bus back to south of the border? The answer is that the authorities have been instructed not to inquire about a family's legal immigration status on purpose or even report it. It goes back to the idea of the government worker having to do too much work again. Perhaps the work they might do isn't any of their legal business anyway. It's a lot easier just to do one's job at hand than open Pandora's Box … Something might fly out that could really get ugly. By keeping the lid on, things stay simple for everybody, or do they? Only on the surface and for a very short time do things stay cool.

Maybe the kids get yanked next time by Protective Investigators. Maybe the overworked construction worker comes home to smack everybody around real good. One day. Maybe he pulls out the gun he has in the dresser drawer in the tiny overcrowded apartment. Then maybe he blows his wife, himself, as well as his kids away to put an end to the American Nightmare that was once his pretty dream. In the end, it's not the bullets that killed, but the greed that infected everyone making up the chain from Latin America to the streets of America, USA Gringolandia.

As usual and like war situations, there are always innocent women and children who pay dearly with their lives to feed greedy men along the path of economic expediency. I can bet that nobody ever thought that by building a condo on the cheap in Miami that it could ever lead to such a bloody mess somewhere on the streets of Little Havana. But, I am sorry to say to all my sports fans, that it really does! We need to wake up and smell the shit that we allow to become part of America. Low wages, lousy working conditions, and illegal, even slave-like conditions for too many people living in the *Greatest Country On the Face of the Earth.*

Can we do any better for ourselves without overturning the apple cart? I say that, of course, we can and surely we must. We must, because the lack of proper and dignified working conditions and humanistic labor laws will only continue to draw us into the morass of economic and social oblivion. To cut to the chase, America will eventually put itself out of business as a world contender and superpower. America could possibly have already taken its first steps toward its decline and fall as did the great Roman Empire. The Roman Empire also became full of many non-Roman citizens, all there in Rome to live the *La Dolce Vita,* or the sweet life.

A place like Miami, is in essence, a prelude to our decline and fall. It is full of aliens, both documented and undocumented. Their presence, ability to be exploited, combined with the greedy local power structure has turned my city into the poorest metropolitan area in the USA. If you want a nice house to clean, come to Miami and work for cash only. If you need to do some day labor so you can work off the street corner, then just come to Miami anytime. Even the tough and independent-spirited taxi drivers of my city work for no salary or any benefits, including workmen's compensation. All the state laws were passed in order to take the employers off the hook legally, by just declaring them all independent contractors. *TAXI –*

I just hope that I am not giving any ideas to the great exploiters of the world by letting out the little dirty secrets of the USA. That would be terrible, if some nasty, mean, and selfish exploiters of greed decided to set up shop in Florida in order to cash in on the lack of proper labor laws. Let's hope that my book can turn things around by shaming our political leaders into cleaning up their act. We do not need more wise guys, but decent guys to locate their businesses in Florida or the South.

The Bible says that we sow what we reap. So if we sow badness, we shall reap misery and our own slide downward. Do we have to emulate the Roman Empire? Must we continue our slide into mediocrity? Personally, I would like to see the USA continue to be the leader of the world in freedom, prosperity, and, most of all, in peace. If we really seek out that more perfect union and are really the great people of faith as we claim, then certainly there is no other choice left. I should think that the alternative is unacceptable to us or any other sane person from whatever other country.

The most perfect example of American legal contradictions and social confusion, combined with social cohesion, is the death penalty issue. Every state has a different way it looks at or enforces their death penalty. Our National Government also is very shaky on its enforcement or lack of enforcement. Sometimes it has been legal to enforce it, and at other times not legal. Recently, the Governor of Illinois took everyone off death row, because he wasn't really sure what to do, considering the dismal error rate in convictions for death row inmates.

Shamefully, I am able to announce that my State of Florida is now number two in our land in its rate of death row executions. Only the big socially backward State of Texas can claim the top spot. Remember that Texas is probably the state with the most illegal working immigrants in the nation as well. Its border shanty towns dot the landscape to accentuate its embrace of the Banana-Republican philosophy of government. Recently a ring of agriculture slaves was broken in Florida and other states, along with rings of slave prostitutes brought in from Mexico. Some of the leaders were arrested and convicted, because not everybody in the USA is a selfish greedy, swine, as you might think.

As you can guess, I am an opponent of the Death Penalty, as are most civilized people of the Book. We now have modern humane methods to keep bad people behind bars for life. Execution is no longer a truly necessary alternative, except for people interested in revenge. "Thou shall not kill" is still one of the Ten Commandments, since I last checked. Are we giving ourselves permission to enforce only the ones we like? That's the way it looks to me, my friends. Has our ability to forgive and turn the other cheek been eradicated by the base instincts associated with killing for revenge?

In the USA we have really strayed from the ancient concept found in the Code of Hammurabi. This Code solidified the concept, centuries ago, that the punishment should fit the crime. But, nowadays with laws like 'three strikes,' a shoplifter can get life in prison. Is that really fair? I personally do not think so. In the USA today, too many people are getting unfair sentences for their crimes. In some cases, they are too lenient, while sometimes they are overly strict. Naturally, all these sentences can vary from state to state, depending upon what's legal or not legal there.

I don't think it's right that somebody can go to jail for three months in one state for spitting on the sidewalk, yet another person in a different state just gets a fine. We need to standardize all our laws for our own future benefit. Our name says it all: the UNITED States of America. We are not the *nonaligned* States of America, yet our hodgepodge of state and national laws reflect it daily.

Guess what country accounts for half of the serial killings in hospitals worldwide? This means that people are being killed while they are in the hospital, by those same hospital staff members hired to heal them. I'll give you three guesses. Is it Nazi Germany, Stalin's Soviet Union, or the USA? O.K., your time has expired. The answer is the USA. That was easy, because you knew that the first two countries no longer exist on paper anymore. Do you find this bit of tragedy so startling or think I am a big, fat liar? Well, I am sad to say as a patriotic America lover that we lead the world in this sad little statistic

So, what is the reason behind this nasty little secret? Is it because we are actually sadistic, mean murderers in America?

No, is the answer to that idea. Actually, the people who get murdered are the result of poor labor laws and Draconian working conditions in our hospitals. It's simple; just do the math. Doctors and nurses have such a large case load of patients today, that the easy way out is to reduce their case load by getting rid of their cases. Hey, it's easy! When your case is dead, then it's no case anymore!

Nobody wants a case load that they can't handle, now do they? Police detectives and State Investigators suffer from the same problem, too. That's why so many crimes like murder always go unsolved. Our governments never give us enough resources and people to really do the job properly. We are muddling through, going through the motions, not giving our best. What we are giving and getting is the minimum effort to keep the entire system barely functioning. We are gradually *ghettoizing* our nation. We are turning the USA into a place where life is cheap and, in too many instances, of no value at all.

The life of an American has been valued by its ability to perform certain economic skills well. Higher money-producing skills, such as pro athletes, rate much higher value than a teacher or a nurse, for example, certainly much higher than a mom and housewife. Anybody can give birth and raise a kid, but not everyone can shoot hoops well. America has way too many moms, but too few home run hitters.

In the end, is a mom who can raise a good son any less valuable to us than Magic Johnson? I say, "no." To me, the mom is a national treasure worthy of the highest accolades and a full time salary for being a mom and housewife, too. What we need are good full-time moms that can dedicate themselves to their children, if they so choose that path. What we do not need are moms who are forced out of the house to work, in order to pay more taxes with their working husbands. Remember that the *double taxation* of families now will never able to keep pace with the ensuing social ills it inadvertently creates. It's really simple. If everybody is working all day, who is watching the kids? Even day care centers and public schools are no substitute for a mom and dad's attention. The Soviet Union and other Communist countries tried to substitute state care and control for family care, and look where they ended up. Most of them are being relegated to the dust heap of historical anomalies.

Is it a cruel joke, or are Americans just really dreaming that we have inadvertently become much like our former Nazi and Communist enemies? I think we have done that very thing. After all, extreme left-wing Communism will eventually meet and blur with extreme right-wing Nazism, as when placed on a circular diagram. In reality, both systems stifle freedom, strive on dictatorship, seek conformity, and constantly look for war as an outlet for sustenance and growth.

Aldous Huxley, in his book Brave New World Revisited, stated the following: *But liberty, as we all know, cannot flourish in a country that is permanently on a war footing, or even a near-war footing. Permanent crisis justifies permanent control of everybody and everything by the agencies of the central government.*

Huxley equated overpopulation and its straining of our natural resources to the level of government control vs. individual freedoms. He predicted that our rapid population growth would become troublesome by the beginning of the 21st century. He predicted this in 1959 when the book Brave New World Revisited was first published. I feel that he was right on target, giving the state of matters in today's USA.

Since the year 1959, the USA has passed through the Cold War, the invasion of the Dominican Republic, the Vietnam War, the War in Grenada, The War in Panama, the War in Somalia, the Gulf War, the War in the Balkans, the War in Afghanistan, and now we face the new *Iraq Attack*. We are presently engaged militarily in Colombia and the Philippines, to boot. We have lost troops all over the globe as in Lebanon, when our Marines were killed by a truck bombing. Let's not forget Yemen, Kuwait, or Saudi Arabia, where our troops were recently killed by assorted sabotage bombings. Our civilians working and traveling abroad are now sitting ducks for any crazy group of saboteurs willing to make a quick name for themselves.

What goes around comes around, and when a nation is on a near-war footing all the time then it opens itself up for all sorts of trouble and retaliation. Is our quest for resources like oil so out of control that we have alienated people who at one time could have been our friends for life? Are we, too, losing the footing of our democratic foundations at the same time, along with the respect of the rest of the world? Has the big boy on the block become the neighborhood bully now? Maybe we are just too young a nation to realize our own strength as compared to the rest of our neighbors.

Sometimes Americans frown on countries that do not have democratic and free elections. We categorize them as totalitarian enemies of the USA and even declare war on them. We try to monitor their elections, teach them how to like us, and be like us. We even write their new Constitutions for them and set up their postwar governments as we did in Japan after WW2. But one thing we never teach these countries is how to have all the rich businessmen from sweeping the elections. Yes, the elections are free and democratic, but money talks and bull shit walks in any election.

One of our allies, King Fahad of Saudi Arabia and by the way also (The Keeper of the Two Holy Mosques) said it all when asked why they do not allow elections in his country. In the word of Fahad: "If we were to have elections, the winners would be rich businessmen who could buy the votes." Maybe he got this idea from watching vote returns from elections in America. Have elections become a rich man's game? Has the voter been relegated to being the pawns in the economic chess match because the unyielding flow of funds goes unchecked? I answer "yes" to both questions, my fellow Americans.

O.K., so now you know the ugly side of political elections in our fragile and young democracy. But is there a solution to the inherent problem or not? Certainly there is: however, the powers that be don't even want to think about it. For not only will it level the playing field for rich and poor candidates, but it will even open a new Pandora's Box of other political parties to have a chance to form and compete against the *Republicrats,* which are our present day Republican and Democrat parties.

American elections are now like a ping pong match, with the same two players always holding the only two rackets, supplying the ping pong balls, and buying the table to share between themselves. Our only two viable political parties even get to keep the keys to the gym where the ping pong matches are always played, so nobody else can even get in when they are not there playing.

But since our political parties do not produce anything themselves, they have to find a legitimate source to finance the matches they hog so well. The solution is easy: get the money from big multinational companies and *fat cat groups* willing to sell their souls for any monetary gains. Set up *legal PAC,* or political action committees to accept the money, to divert the legalized bribery away from the direct hands of the candidates. Allow the candidates to get *small potatoes money* from local contributors, so as not to appear to be taking money for favors. Remember, as long as it is legal on paper, it is legal in the USA. Morality does not enter into the picture, unfortunately. This so-called legality allows us to criticize other third world countries as in Latin America, by referring to them as corrupt *Banana Republics.* Places like Latin America are very easy for us to mock as corrupt from top to bottom, their leaders pictured as bribe-taking, and palm greasing opportunists. Our constant criticism of other, smaller, and weaker countries somehow makes us feel better, and also takes off the heat from our slimy system of campaign finance. When you turn on the news, it's always very common to get headlines about other countries' social and political problems that *of course* don't exist at home. Recently, headlines were all over the political corruption scandals from Mexico, for example. A former Mexican president's brother was hunted down by the press about his bribery and secret Swiss bank accounts. Why do we take so much interest in what goes on in somebody else's house, when our own home is also full of garbage? Why do we always say that somebody else's shit stinks so badly, if we can't even smell our own? It's because, by constant denial, the problem does not exist. Ask any mentally dysfunctional person that's in denial to try to get any professional help. It is almost impossible to do so. Alcoholics Anonymous knows that the first step on the long road to full recovery is for the person to admit fully that he is an alcoholic and has no true control over his disease.

When we admit as a nation that we are also afflicted by a disease, then and only then shall we ever recover our moral and political strength once again. Our disease is the affliction of greed! We are greedy for the material advantages that money brings. But our greed for power is also at the root of it as well, for politics offers the duality of power and money. The two can not be easily separated. Only therapy and the willingness to reform our nasty habits can save us. But a nation's political system is not the same as a sick alcoholic, though some of our politicians have been known to be afflicted by the drink as well.

The two easiest ways to cure the political patient are with <u>limited access to money and term limits for all elected positions</u> at all levels of government nation-<u>wide.</u> All candidates for public office must be given exactly the same amount of money to spend on their campaign. The money would come from our taxes, as is partially done now for presidential elections. This way any *Joe Blow* that can qualify legally as a candidate will get the same chance as the rich guy from the downtown law firm with the right connections. All candidates need to be finger-printed and checked for prior convictions, just like we do now for almost any responsible job. This should reduce the *wise guys* looking to get elected quite considerably.

Also, by putting strict limits on the terms of office, many power hungry and overly materialistic slime balls will think twice before they want to take on the public trust. They will realize that they won't be able to get entrenched, in order to set up any corrupt political dynasty. Today, many of these political dynasties are handed down to their sons and daughters OOPS! Did I strike a nerve here?

Once strict term limits and tougher qualifying laws are in place, we then need to give all political parties the same chance for funding. Any party, no matter how small its core base has got to have the chance to play in the great *Republicratic* ping pong match that is presently our election system. Even a party with one or two percent of the total political sphere should be able to get a shot at the chance to win a game or two.

This financing of political parties can be done easily on everyone's tax return yearly. All you would have to do is earmark a certain percentage to the party of one's choice, with a maximum allowed by law for each and every taxpayer. This would completely get rid of PAC and direct contributions to candidates. Nobody running for office would even know who actually gave him the money. It would be up to each party to run its slate of candidates and spend the money as they saw fit. This way, whoever ran the best campaign and slated the best field of candidates would probably have the best chance to win their elections.

Since all parties candidates would have term limits, the voting public could actually look at some tangible results over a set period of time, rather than over a period of never ending ping pong matches, where the scores either aren't kept, or are secrets between the two participants. It would be now a case of party results talk and shitty parties walk. This is a lot better than the alternative we now have of money talks, period! For once we have people who desire public office to help people they are not directly related to once again, we shall have a nation of fully functioning, patriotic citizens who care about one another for the common good. No one would ever dare to rip off the taxpayers or pull a political fast one, enabling him to line his pockets.

If we have the balls to criticize countries like Mexico for their one-party monopoly, their undemocratic shady tricks, let's put our house in order by loosening the *republicratic* strangle hold which is cutting off any meaningful change in government and society. Remember, we are here to form "A More Perfect Union" as our forefathers stated over two hundred years ago. We are not here to see ourselves go down the tubes of economic and political oblivion for want of change caused by the conventional wisdom of economic expediency and the political survival of charlatans.

In the USA it is not so easy to move from one state to another without going through some sort of economic and social upheaval and inconvenience, especially for professionals. Every state has its own standards and regulations for professional licensing in fields like law, accounting, education, nursing, and medicine. Somebody who wants to move to a new state to practice his trade might not be able to do so as easily as he may think. Even if he gets a position rapidly, it is usually on a provisional basis until he passes the new state's requirements for licensing, testing, and education ...

Teacher certification, in particular, is a particularly cumbersome process in most states, let alone when a certified teacher in one state wants to teach in another state. State bureaucracy is so overly <u>entrenched</u> at present that if a teacher doesn't stay certified in his home state on a continuous basis, he will completely lose it, and have to begin the whole process all over from the beginning.

It <u>behooves</u> us to establish national standards for all professions that require any sort of state certification or licensing. Why should a person have to risk economic hardship and insecurity, just because he wants to live in a different state? It just doesn't make sense economically and socially for our nation to go on treating people from different states as if they were really from another country. But, in essence this is exactly what we are presently doing to our professional class of citizens.

In actuality, the most important thing that a state should do if somebody wants to become a professional in a new state is to check their criminal background thoroughly. This would automatically take out the dishonest and dangerous players immediately, before they had a chance to do any damage in their new states of residence. If a teacher with experience and good references decides to move to a new state, why should he have to be retested, reeducated, and reevaluated as if he were a new kid on the block? National teacher certification standards could put an end to this *'business of education'* almost overnight.

Unfortunately, education has become a big business, controlled by state politicians and bureaucrats. However, it is not actually the real feed bag for them that one might think. They surely benefit with their high salaries, kickbacks, and freebies, but the big money is in the contracts awarded to the big fish servicing the actual institutions and school districts. Nowadays, everybody and their brother has their hand out reaching for the big tasty pies represented by large school districts and state universities.

In large school districts as in Miami-Dade County, sometimes you can't even tell the good guys from the bad guys. Union officials work with lobbyists under the table in order to get kickbacks on insurance contracts for their members. They even go on to endorse private charter schools, where public money goes into the hands of private companies set up by state and local politicians and cronies. They just make sure that their state certified union members get the new jobs.

Sometimes you even get Miami-Dade School Board members directly benefiting themselves by their open business relationships, either directly or indirectly with the school system. We once had a guy on the board that had an exclusive deal to peddle *school insurance* to the parents for their children attending the system's schools. He finally retired and faded into oblivion, rich as a Southern fried fat cat.

Another case involved a fellow who got a resolution passed by the board to force school uniforms down everybody's throats. You guessed it! He happened to own a school uniform business in Miami. He was later forced off the board due to criminal charges against him related to housing fraud on some rental property he owned. The man's son ran an unsuccessful bid to replace his dad, after it was learned the he really did not live in the school district he represented in the election.

Only God knows what really goes on in all of our nation's school districts and institutions of higher learning, for my brief insight is just the tip of the iceberg, slowly melting around us. My point here is to emphasize that the education of our children or adults is not for economic profit or the enrichment of the overly materialistic peddlers of schlock. It is rather for the overall benefit of American society and our future welfare as the continued leaders of the free world.

How can we continue to remain on top if the very foundation of our citizens' education is eroded and dulled by corrupt self-serving institutions of business working in cahoots with bootlicking members of government? The answer is that we can't. For this reason, today we are in short supply of many sorts of professionals at home: nursing, medicine, science, and engineering are just a few to be mentioned. Young American professionals are shying away from these areas at an ever-alarming rate. Once they get a taste of the nasty working conditions they must endure, they head for the door. Sometimes our brightest youngsters don't even bother to jump through all the hoops at all and go into fields that don't require so much of a hassle economically, psychically, or emotionally.

One of the professions in America with possibly the widest variance and most nonstandardized work scenario is that of Police Officer. All across our nation, these standards for entrance and completion of the time honored profession vary as wildly as do species of cannabis-sativa plants all over the world. Some police departments are looking for really intelligent people with college degrees, while others look for the dullest they can find with only a high school education. Crime fighting takes the best minds not the most mediocre. A four-year college degree should be the starting point for any police work anywhere in America today.

There have been cases where people who score too high on the police entrance exam tests are automatically disqualified from further consideration. This happened in a particular New England Police Department, so the applicant sued to get hired. You would think the court would support his desire to become a policeman, but for some reason it did not. The court sided with the police department, saying the department had the right to not hire an intelligent person if it wanted. The department in question feared that if an applicant were too intelligent, he may get too easily bored on the job and quit: thereby wasting the money which was used to train him.

Perhaps the problem of possible job boredom lies in the fact that organizations full of average-mediocre staff cause the whole police process to screech to a dull and boring halt. Crime-solving takes brains and imagination, rather than dull-witted prodding. If an intelligent person were up against the blue wall of dullards, he would certainly find himself going nowhere fast and making a hell of a lot of enemies along the way. Nobody likes a wise guy anyway, especially a superior officer with seniority.

I once saw an episode of the Twilight Zone on TV where children of the future were given IQ tests. They were to be put to death by the state, if they scored too high, rather than too low. Is this what our country is coming to? Are we becoming afraid of people who are too intelligent? Are intelligent people a threat to our organizational structures so touted as some of the best in the world? The answer is "yes". We are, as organizations, suspicious of people who act just a little too smart for *our* own good. Smart people are generally seen as a threat to the entire fabric of organizations and specifically the top level managers who run them. Managers, after all, usually have an IQ level just above average at best. Remember, they are hired as employees because they are not smart or creative enough to make their own companies or businesses. When a smarter person comes along to make suggestions, he is greatly feared by them. Managers are in the end only really interested in their jobs, not the bottom lines of their respective companies or government organizations.

Intelligent people today are at a distinct disadvantage, especially when they go for a job interview. In order to just get through the first hurdles, they must sublimate their brains to the lower levels of the interview process. They must learn how to dumb down, use pat answers and catch phrases now being touted by career growth experts. For once anything else but the mediocre is seen or even suspected, the *smart ass* is dead in the water.

It's no wonder that our nation is now having to import people from other countries, as well-paid slaves in order to do jobs that should be done by intelligent home grown Americans. There are really two reasons this is being done nowadays. The first is to save money on salaries; an Indian or Pakistani needs less than an American, to be sure. The next reason is to keep the chain on the new organizational monkey through a process of visa grantings or yankings, depending upon circumstances. Someone in the USA on a series of temporary work related visas is much more willing to work harder and kiss a hell of a lot more organizational butt than a plain old smart-ass American.

This particular point brings me to give a good example of exactly just this unpatriotic and very un-American phenomenon. It's the cruise line industry. Next time you take a cruise from one of our safe, sanitary, and well-organized ports, I dare you to find more than a handful of Americans actually working on one of the ships you may board. Americans are normally found working as entertainers or shipboard cruise directors, and even then a Canadian will suffice if one can be found to work cheaper.

So, you ask yourself how such an obvious and blatant disregard of *the rules* could be allowed to happen, and even flourish. The answer goes back to my brief insight into campaign financing laws in the USA. Our politicians are legally allowing it to happen everyday and everywhere in America. They are simply taking the money from these cruise line people to bend the rules and allow everything they want to happen, which by the way includes nonpayment of US corporate income taxes. Campaign contributions are so delicious and nonfattening; they are irresistible to any politicians. Could you imagine a whole cruise ship full of American employees? Well, my lord! They might just try to unionize to avoid the 16-hour days now endured by most TCN's (third country nationals) who now ply the seas on assorted love boats and fun ships.

These international conglomerates, which are mainly American-based and financed, sell their stocks on our stock markets to get more money to literally keep afloat. Without our investments, liberal (wink, wink) laws, and the millions of tourists we provide them, they'd be out of gas tomorrow. Well, of course they do pay some fees and taxes to our governments, but the lion's share in taxes, decent salaries, benefits to American families, and in the end your real safety aboard, will continue to escape us as a nation.

If our standard of living keeps going down for lack of decent employment, who will fill the cruise ships we now put to sea from places like Miami? If we are not wanted to work on the cruise ships, maybe some day we won't be able to travel on them. Maybe our wages in the USA will get so low that the cruise lines will have to cut prices to the point that even they won't make enough money to stay out of bankruptcy in the end. Remember the saying from the Spanish: *Lo barato sale caro*. This means that going it on the cheap turns out very expensive. This simple saying, if taken to heart, can save the USA from its continuous preoccupation for eternal cost-cutting and penny pinching when human beings who happen to be Americans are concerned.

We deserve better consideration from our own politicians than we are currently getting at present. Our money is financing guys who could care less about you, your chances for a job, or even the safety of your family. There is so much disparity of pay all over the USA that the gap between the rich and the poor is widening, due to the overzealous and greedy pro-business laws that are awash in a sea of love boats. But not all states have so strong anti-people laws. There are still places with good-hearted patriotic, honest politicians who make sure their constituents make decent living wages.

The great disparity in pay from state to state is undermining the social stability of our nation. We have rich states like New York and California, while we have poor states like Mississippi and Florida. Poorer states are found to have low levels of education, skills, and real economic opportunity for their citizens. Non-unionized minimum wage states are full of crime, family meltdowns, drug use, alcoholism, and gambling, which is even encouraged now by the states in which they live. They call it the state lottery, but Ben Franklin just called it a tax for fools.

The stability of our various levels of American governments is hard to match. But in my opinion they have become stagnated by their penchant for inflexible mazes of bureaucratic red tape, overloaded with doses of nepotistic corruption and inefficiency. Our American brothers and sisters are falling through the cracks in under-funded and deliberately understaffed agencies legally set up to care for them. If we are going to try to replace the family and church structures of charity and caring with the Department of Children and Families, we better be sure it's supplied with what it needs to save those families and children from ugly, unwanted scenarios later down the road.

Public elementary schools have become baby-sitting like holding cells for children while high schools have become detention centers, so the cops don't have to worry about the teenage kids during the day. Nothing scares a cop more than thinking of summer vacation for public school students. Can you imagine all the break-ins and car crashes they would have to contend with if it weren't for school time? Besides being really big business, the idea of *In loco parentis*, where teachers have taken the authority of parents for the day appeals to everybody, except maybe to most of the students. Once the states decided to replace parents to solve their kid's problems with state certified teachers and other assorted educators, it really bit off much more than it could ever chew. We are talking money-wise and socially-wise as well.

Teachers are supposed to be equal to parents for the day, but everyone knows this is not even really close to the truth. If a teacher ever does what a parent does to his own kid, his days as an educator are severely numbered. What educators have become are Nazi-like mandatory reporters to law enforcement, should it be discovered that a child is in harm's way from members of his own family.

The real elements of change in American education are taking a back seat to the perpetuation of the status quo in governments everywhere. Greed, in the form of politicians without term limits, unchecked funds when shaken and stirred with dashes of school board contractors-administrators are having their run of the bulls all over the USA. But the bulls do trample and even kill while let loose to run the streets. It appears that the teachers of America are seriously getting gored as the bulls are allowed to run freely. Our teachers are the gored and bloody scapegoats for the ills of our public schools.

How much longer is America to blame our teachers for its own problems? We are talking family-based, severely dysfunctional kinds of problems, where no parents are even around to see to it that Johnny gets home safely after a stressful day at school. What has happened here is that our mostly lawyer-politicians have used education as their personal ax to grind to garner votes for themselves and their cohorts. If we blame the teachers, we in turn take the direct heat off the families with the kids that are supposedly putting the politicos in office in the first place. But let us never forget that teachers have kids and families as well. However, you'd never know it from listening to the deafening noise created by the sharpening of axes, the same ones used to chop the states' budgets in the never-ending crescendo to save tax dollars, all at the expense of America's nebulous future. Remember; *lo barato sale caro*. Being cheap with teachers and schools today will continue to produce a further speeding up in the dumbing down process of America.

But I guess that is O.K. too, since we can always keep importing the *smart people* from places like India and China, to do the real brainy work our own kids either can't or don't want to do. By the way, countries like Germany are also presently experiencing the same phenomenon. Companies like BMW are constantly on the look out for *smart people* to work as engineers and designers at their facilities in Munich for exactly the same reasons. German young people are unwilling to sacrifice what it takes to do the really brainy work. The German School *Systems* have drifted away from science and math toward the liberal arts arena.

I have to hand it to the Germans for their excellent planning skills. They have seen the future and were prepared. German schools abound in places like South America, where children who enter primary school are speaking like Goebbels by the time they graduate high school. They also are taught English to boot, so they can compete with us in the ever shrinking global marketplace. How many American kids do you know that can speak three languages fluently by the time they finish High School? I know kids from places like Colombia and Ecuador who can run mental circles around most American High School graduates. Let's not even mention places like India and China once again, for fear of embarrassment.

We can do better than that if we only try half as hard in education as we do in military development or space exploration. America's education system could be a heck of a lot better and we know it. Our overworked teachers slugging it out in overcrowded classrooms can tell you that firsthand. Most new teachers usually do not make it more than five years before they quit in absolute horror. Community colleges and the like now are forced to hire very qualified people on a part time basis only (This means no benefits and absolutely no job security for some of our most intelligent and dedicated individuals.) Is this really the best we can do in order to form a more perfect union? You know the answer to that one, my fellow Americans (LBJism). That stands for Lyndon Baines Johnson, our President who declared a War on Poverty so many moons ago.

If we can win in Iraq today, why can't we win in America tomorrow? Do we need to invade the schools of America, just to get them on the right track? Will we learn to think along avenues of peace, rather than along plans of war, to turn around our most vicious problems at home? Once America stops whitewashing problems in schools in order to make its administrators look good, we will have taken the first step on a long road back from mediocrity. We will be walking toward real improvement in education and as a society as a whole.

Our strength as a nation lies not in its bombs or missiles of today, but its children's futures. Please, do not stop to tell me that without the military overkill, our kids would have no future at all. I simply do not buy into that big lie syndrome, put out by the military-industrial complex. We were warned about this happening by President and former General Eisenhower, as he left office in 1961. We did not listen then, because the Cold War perpetuated by those very groups of people didn't allow us.

Americans had a great life after WW2, with a new prosperity never seen before. It was easy for us to get seduced by the big cars and cheeseburgers. But because we had it so well, we never bothered to peer into the future as the Germans did, as they were forced to rebuild from the ashes of war. A *true lasting power* never allows itself to get into the overall social and economic malaise we currently find ourselves.

I got an e-mail from one of my old friends from Texas, a learned individual with advanced degrees from East Coast Schools. I feel that "The Arrogance of Power", written by Senator Robert C. Byrd of West Virginia says a lot of what I feel and have written about, regarding what's wrong with America.

"I believe in this beautiful country. I have studied its roots and gloried in the wisdom of its magnificent Constitution. I have marveled at the wisdom of its founders and framers. Generation after generation of Americans has understood the lofty ideals that underlie our great Republic. I have been inspired by the story of their sacrifice and their strength.

But, today I weep for my country. I have watched the events of recent months with a heavy, heavy heart. No more is the image of America one of strong, yet benevolent peace keeper. The image of America has changed. Around the globe, our friends mistrust us, our word is disputed, and our intentions are questioned.

Instead of reasoning with those with whom we disagree, we demand obedience or threaten recrimination. Instead of isolating Saddam Hussein, we seem to have isolated ourselves. We proclaim a new doctrine of preemption which is understood by few and feared by many. We say that the United States has the right to turn its firepower on any corner of the globe which might be suspect in the war on terrorism. We assert that right without the sanction of any international body. As a result, the world has become a much more dangerous place.

We flaunt our superpower status with arrogance. We treat UN Security Council members like ingrates who offend our princely dignity by lifting their heads from the carpet. Valuable alliances are split. After war has ended, the United States will have to rebuild much more than the country of Iraq. We will have to rebuild America's image around the globe.

The case this Administration tries to make to justify its fixation with war is tainted by charges of falsified documents and circumstantial evidence. We cannot convince the world of the necessity of this war for one simple reason. This is a war of choice.

There is no credible information to connect Saddam Hussein to 9/11. The twin towers fell because a worldwide terrorist group, Al Qaeda, with cells in over 60 nations, struck at our wealth and our influence by turning our own planes into missiles, one of which would likely have slammed into the dome of this beautiful Capitol except for the brave sacrifice of the passengers on board.

The brutality seen on September 11th and in other terrorist attacks we have witnessed around the globe are the violent and desperate efforts by extremists to stop the daily encroachment of western values upon their cultures. That is what we fight. It is a force not confined to borders. It is a shadowy entity with many faces, many names, and many addresses.

But this Administration has directed all of the anger, fear, and grief which emerged from the ashes of the twin towers and the twisted metal of the Pentagon towards a tangible villain, one we can see and hate and attack; and villain he is. But he is the wrong villain; and this is the wrong war. If we attack Saddam Hussein, we will probably drive him from power. But the zeal of our friends to assist our global war on terrorism may have already taken flight.

The general unease surrounding this war is not just due to "orange alert." There is a pervasive sense of rush and risk and too many questions unanswered. How long will we be in Iraq? What will be the cost? What is the ultimate mission? How great is the danger at home? A pall has fallen over the Senate Chamber. We avoid our solemn duty to debate the one topic on the minds of all Americans, even while scores of thousands of our sons and daughters faithfully do their duty in Iraq.

What is happening to this country? When did we become a nation which ignores and berates our friends? When did we decide to risk undermining international order by adopting a radical and doctrinaire approach to using our awesome military might? How can we abandon diplomatic efforts when the turmoil in the world cries out for diplomacy?

Why can this President not seem to see that America's true power lies not in its will to intimidate, but in its ability to inspire?

War appears inevitable. But I continue to hope that the cloud will lift. Perhaps Saddam will yet turn tail and run. Perhaps reason will somehow still prevail. I, along with millions of Americans, will pray for the safety of our troops, for the innocent civilians in Iraq, and for the security of our homeland. May God continue to bless the United States of America in the troubled days ahead, and may we somehow recapture the vision which for the present eludes us."

There is an old Jewish saying that goes something like this: **If three men tell you that you are drunk, then you should lie down.** I think this sums it up for the USA with regard to our decision to finally invade Iraq after the Senator's warning. The entire world has begged us to be prudent, but we did not listen because we did not believe we were *drunk with power*. When you are too drunk to know it and don't lie down, you are asking for trouble and will surely get it.

The Senator's first question, How long will we be in Iraq? appears to be based upon our determination to grab and control the natural resources of the country. After all, everybody knows that a nation with the second largest oil reserves must be a very good reason to look at Saddam and his government with such microscopic precision. Other nations in Africa and Latin America, for example, without the oil somehow go unnoticed while their brutal dictatorships are allowed to flourish.

In my estimation, we are there for the long haul, that is, if we can stand having to keep the peace among all the warring factions inside Iraq that Saddam managed to control so well under his brutalizing dictatorship. Let's just hope that we do not replace Saddam as the new *bad guys*, who people like Osama Bin Laden has been warning the Muslims about for so long. The trap is set now, and we are on the brink of falling right into the net, as we have done so many times in the past all over the globe.

Senator Byrd also asked about the costs, and so far it is at least 80 billion dollars and rising. You and I pay for this in the way of more taxes, less public services, slow economic progress, lay-offs, and future problems that will be the result of current social issues going ignored right now. Wars only really create death and destruction. They bring temporary economic stimulus with a disregard for the welfare of the American social future. The true cost of any war can never be measured in the end in true dollars and cents. However, you can be sure the bottom lines of the Military-Industrial Complex concerns will be sweet and fat each and every time they can get our Congress to allow a war to proceed as usual.

The Senator asks about the ultimate mission. That appears to be the control of the natural resources of Iraq by installing an American puppet government, as we did in Viet Nam and in so many other places in Latin America. This also means billions in contracts for companies linked to the military for so many years. You can already hear the pigs at the trough, snorting for position. These are the same players already in places like Saudi Arabia, where their employees live like Sultans.

Senator Byrd also asks about the danger at home as well. However, the danger at home is a two edged sword. By protecting ourselves from further terrorism, we also lose the last vestiges of real freedom we have left at home. These lost freedoms could be the right to bear arms, the right to assemble freely, freedom of religion, and, of course, freedom of the press; which is always the first to go in a police state or a country on a constant war footing or near war footing (George Orwell).

I do not think that freedom-loving Americans really want this to happen, yet if we delude ourselves into thinking that an invasion of some country will be better for our security we are playing with fire. Sure 9/11 needs to be taken seriously, but not at the cost of waking up in an America we do not recognize anymore. American desires for basic natural resources, needed to feed our economic powers, is no excuse for destroying the very things that made us the greatest country on the face of the Earth.

Social Regimentation in America:

Regimentation of people is something that is necessary for military discipline and effective battle plans. It is effective in achieving its goals for the military, yet it is not something we should strive for in civilian society. But that is exactly what the USA has been doing almost since the last shot was fired in WW2.

The military based *Chain of Command* has crept into all aspects of civilian employment. Private companies, and especially government, have been taken over by such entrenched military structures. When I first took a job with the State of Florida, I immediately noticed the marked similarities in 1972. I felt that I was back in the Army ROTC, sans the uniform. State supervisors were like my former military superiors. The man who interviewed me for the job was a retired WW2 officer and was very suspicious of someone like me, as I was a former conscientious objector to the Viet Nam War. He hired me anyway, because he liked the fact that I was an Anglo-American, fluent in Spanish. At the time, Spanish was a requirement for the position and I guess they did not want to have to hire a Hispanic unless it was absolutely necessary.

Social regimentation breaks the creative and imaginary spirit of the individual and even can instill fear to take risks. These are qualities we need to continue to stay on top as a great nation. Risk taking and creativity are what made us so powerful to begin with. The American Revolution was a very great risk to take against the entrenched British Kingdom. Our creativity in battle and politics against them allowed us to find the freedom we so cherish today.

Today, however, even our public school systems are models of an ineffective social quagmire, brought on by the social regimentation, so well modeled after our military institutions. We are winning the battles in Iraq right now, but losing the war on poverty at home as people considered inadaptable for our social settings continue to fall between the cracks. We have no social net for our civilian casualties. Some of our fellow Americans, if only given the right tools and a real break, can make it at home and regain their family skills once again. Too many people wander the streets of America today for anyone to deny we don't have big problems.

If no American soldiers' bodies are left wounded or dead in Iraq, why should we allow civilian *social casualties* at home to be treated worse? After all, aren't our soldiers fighting for our civilians' well being at home and the fabulous way of life we so tout? If not, why should they fight at all? The military categorizes some soldiers as *inadaptable for military service*, when they just don't fit in somehow. Since our civilian institutions have become *militarized* too, we are now finding ourselves full of inadaptable people in all areas of civilian life as well.

A perfect example of this is in teaching, where real-risk taking and creativity are thrown out the window of the very classroom they're in. Rigid lesson plans combined with *in the box* teaching strategies have made good teachers either leave the system or become state-sponsored lackeys and mule team drivers. Corporate America isn't far off the same mark. They seem to look for people who ask no questions and make no creative waves. It's no wonder that bankruptcies are at an all-time high, as corporate misdeeds have almost put a halt to investor confidence in the Stock Market.

Our economic miracles and progress in the USA has unfortunately also produced many civilian casualties. These are those poor souls who have been either turned off mentally or actually been made sick in both body and soul. They are of no great use to the machines of economic and social stimulation that make America the strongest and largest economic engine in the world. These are the kinds of people who are working either beneath their true potential, or else just have decided not to work at all. They subsist or exist on the fringes, perhaps to be found as members of the *Gray Economy*, where so many dropouts or even so called outcasts have been forced to go.

These disenchanted Americans started out with noble goals and aspirations, that fit into the standard goals everyone usually has by the time they finish school. But somewhere along the way to achievement of their goals, something like a brick wall of numbing stagnation called *social regimentation* hit them so hard that they were down for the count. The bell was sounded to let them know it was over, but their ears could not hear the sound. They never expected the blow to be so hard, so fast, and seemingly come out of nowhere, to knock them off their naive little feet.

To numb the pains, our brothers and sisters revert to substance abuse and the vicious cycle of on again-off again feel good days. Since they are so inadaptable to *service*, these potentially very valuable members of American Society find little hope for their recuperation. The entrance back into the society which shuns them as a productive member looks very bleak, if not impossible all together. Second chances are scarce for people who *mess up* in America, just like in the military structure we have so inadvertently adapted to our civilian lives.

If our armed forces are so good at killing and conquering others, and we can build up other nations so well, when are we going to learn when and how to conquer our own foibles and fears at home? I say the time is right now. As soon as you put this book down, why don't you do some small peaceful act that could help us to continue to be the greatest nation on the face of the Earth? Let's continue to strive to be that more perfect union we desire.

Government stability is paramount in America, yet we are now inadvertently taking the stability out of our nation by our narrow-minded *present only* thinking. We need to look far into the future by seeing the realities of our present dilemmas. If we continue not to conveniently see them, our future securities are surely to be questioned. When an open sore is left to heal on its own, the possibility of complications may set in. Some sort of guiding hand would surely help to heal it.

Our society, without the guiding hands of caring, patriotic Americans can only lead to infectious problems.

The stronger the military gets, the more it takes away from the strength of our social fiber. Right now it is so powerful that the future social health and stability of the USA is coming into question daily. People at home are in the streets begging, hawking water, sleeping under bridges, strung out, dying from AIDS, or have even had to join the military as a last resort to survive into the future. Nobody has to put a gun to somebody's head to join the military, simply because in so many situations it's the only socially viable option left for them.

The all volunteer military appears to have created the employment vacuum in which so many educated people have found themselves. For every slot the military needs to fill, it kills a job in the civilian work force. Recruiters are now so brazen as to have begun their recruitment efforts in the public schools, having formed Jr. ROTC brigades. When I say that civilian slots are killed, it's because it's so impossible for most employers to compete with the cradle-to-grave benefits offered by our military structures. But, let's not forget who is really paying for those juicy enticing work packages. We are paying with our tax dollars and we continue to pay more each year as the monolithic structures proliferate throughout peacetime. Do you know of anywhere else except in the military, where you can get a nice retirement package after 20 years, which by the way includes free medical treatment for life?

A truly capitalist society couldn't have figured out a better way then to have sewn the seeds of its own demise so well After all, if free-market employment is made to take a back-seat to government sponsored gravy trains, how can it remain healthy or even have much hope for economic survival? The answer is that it can not, and should not either. I do not think our founding fathers meant that a *well regulated militia* means an overstuffed permanent standing army overseas somewhere. The military shrinks and deters true capitalist growth, not stimulate it in the long run. The money spent on recruitment-to-grave could well be diverted to where it's more required for the future health of our nation. That means places like schools, hospitals, elder care, housing, and the general welfare of our citizenry. Whatever somebody truly needs to make his life in America healthy, successful, and happy should always take priority over the bombs and bullets. Unfortunately, the *guns and butter* philosophy prevalent in America has lost sight of the butter, and I for one do not like the taste of margarine too much.

If somebody wants to get clean of drugs and has no insurance coverage to do so effectively, he can't even join the military. But, if he gets hooked after he joins up with the military, he's covered. Somehow, I can't see the difference. If it is the ultimate mission of our military personnel to protect our civilian-democratic institutions, to protect the Constitution and its citizenry, why can't some guy with not enough money to see a doctor get the same noble treatment? He should in my humble opinion, yet he isn't in today's America.

When single mothers are nowadays being taken prisoner of war in places like Iraq, we have taken a turn in the wrong direction as a viable power of the future. Not only do small children need their moms to be home with them, but they need them to stay alive as well long into the future as grandmothers. Mothers are being indirectly forced from their homes out into the ever-shrinking job market, a job market that pays wages that haven't kept pace with inflation for years. Many of these moms are hearing the sounds of the military vacuum cleaner hoses, sucking them right into harm's way. They can now wind up almost anyplace in the world, to be killed or taken as a POW. I pity the poor kids whose mothers go missing or are killed in action. Their futures are in serious doubt and their cost to Americans to go undetermined, too.

Desperate times at home have produced desperate actions for so many young people faced with economic hardships or a supposed *easy way out*. But in the end, no military sacrifice has ever been easy or even close to being a free ride for its participants. The loss of personal freedom or one's life in the end is rarely worth it. Freedom comes not from giving in to the big wave of regimentation and obedience. It comes from the ability of the individual to have options available to unlock his full potential for economic and social progress. But if the money is not there for our civilians, the choices evaporate rapidly.

The two-paycheck husband-wife work scenario is what has let our military inspired government expand so rapidly. The strategy was simple. Get mom out the door, pay her a lot less than her husband to do the same work, and collect the extra taxes for expanded government expenditures. This simple idea is flawed to really work in the end. It is loaded with all sorts of social land mines and booby traps either unforeseen or totally ignored by its implementers. The social fallout in the way of billions spent to keep it going seems hardly worth the experiment now. Divorce, crime, dumbing down, crumbling infrastructures, as well as the loss of our Judeo-Christian values seem too high a price to pay.

As a fifth grader in Miami, I can still remember a very special teacher, Mr. Rosenberg, who began the class each day with the reading of a psalm from the Holy Bible. He happened to be Jewish, which was a rarity at that time for public school teachers in Miami. I think he was the very first Jewish teacher ever for me. The class was composed of mostly Christian children; however it did contain quite a few Jewish kids as well. A different pupil was called upon to read a psalm each day after we recited the pledge of allegiance to our flag. I can remember it being a time when I was very happy and very proud of who I was.

Everybody basically got along well together and came from a two-parent household, as I did. The only thing different from today would be the fact that our schools were not integrated yet, as the Deep South mentality still ruled the roost in Florida. Sometimes you'd get the Jew-baiting from some of the Southern kids who had come from places like Georgia or Tennessee. But the Jewish kids were tough, because their parents were survivors from places like Europe or the South Bronx. Most of the time, the Jewish kids could either talk their way out or punch their way out if necessary. The David and Goliath story from the Old Testament really helped to give a lot of extra power to the Jewish kids somehow, I guess.

Our Judeo-Christian values and world were intact and when we went home at 3PM, at least our moms were there waiting for us, instead of out having to make money like moms do today. Today, too many kids come from divorced parents or really never meet their father, at all and live with people not related to them. The state has taken over the role of the family in too many instances and failed miserably overall.

The extra money generated by working moms for taxes can never make up for the expenditures needed to clean up the family breakup mess we now find ourselves in today. The real strength of the USA is not to be measured in dollars and cents, but in the integrity and strength of its families. If we use the family as the true measuring stick, I n I am afraid that we are quite ill as a nation. I do not accept notions that the nontraditional family is ever as good for kids as the best traditional family organization. Ozzie and Harriett style family scenarios are based upon the Biblical standards set forth in our Judeo-Christian faiths. The Muslim faith as well embraces this family format for example.

The idea of *Living in Sin*, as the norm for child-rearing, is a great setback to our foundations of the two-parent family structure, which bore this nation and continues to hold it on track against all odds. Of course, there are times when a man and woman should call it quits. Divorce is a necessary matter at times even when children are concerned, but perhaps if more effort was made for couples to attend mandatory counseling before divorcing, we'd have less of it overall. Marriage is no easy ride for anyone, and it takes tremendous amounts of effort and work to see it succeed. Americans have unfortunately become too unrealistic in this regard, perhaps expecting easy story book-like marriages. The ease in which divorces are granted, along with unrealistic expectations, have led to a rise in divorce and a decline in its popularity. People just have to look at the statistics and decline taking the plunge. Then what we get is a generation of kids born out of wedlock and have moms without dads who need to work outside the home. Latchkey kids are created for schools bursting at the seams to try and handle. But the military gets the money needed for them, and all hell begins to break loose.

Remember that we can't have our cake and eat it, too. We can't put kids on the street and expect them to be O.K. everyday without the proper **supervision** and **love** so greatly lacking presently, in the greatest country on the face of the Earth. Government and military growth is all well and good as long as our homeland defense is in defense of our most sensitive and vulnerable members of society. I am talking about our moms, kids, grandparents, dads, uncles and aunts, who together make up what's really all we have in the end.

THE PEACE BROKE OUT:

America has found itself in one sort of cold or hot war since its inception. Sometimes it was necessary for its very survival, but other times for economic self-interest instead. At this juncture in time, I feel we are looking for problems as a muscle-bound teenager looks for a fight to test his strength. Going around beating up bad guys can be a tricky act to continue forever, because we could get the reputation as being a bully if we are not more careful. We should not wage war on others if we can't even win our own internal wars we have declared upon ourselves. Here we can use the War on Poverty and the War on Drugs as two perfect examples of lost causes at home. We still have lots of drugs in the USA and lots of poverty.

If Americans can't lick our homegrown wars, let's not be so quick to invade and bully smaller, less potent countries either. Our energy and money could be better spent at home first. Matthew Chapter 7 verse 3 states the following: "And why do you look at the speck in your brother's eye, but do not consider the plank in your own eye?" I feel we have strayed and forgotten these words of wisdom, so simply put, yet so powerful a message to all Americans.

Riches can be brought from arms dealing and war. The military-industrial complex presently strangling our families and nation from future growth grows richer and bigger everyday. Timothy, verses 9 and 10 states the following: "But _Bible_ those who desire to be rich fall into temptation and a snare, and *into* many foolish and harmful lusts which drown men in destruction and perdition. For the love of money is a root of *all kinds of evil*, for which some have strayed from the faith in their greediness, and pierced themselves through with many sorrows." Verse 11 gives us the solution to this mess, in which America now finds itself: "But you, O man of God, flee these things and pursue righteousness, godliness, faith, love patience, gentleness."

Along with this glorification of war syndrome America suffers from, we have also been affected by its paramilitary consequences. Just turn on the TV to see new shows about all sorts of policemen, from FBI to CSI, from The Agency to NYPD. These Americans are the good guys, but let's not forget that a healthy civilian society should not venerate them, either. We run the risk of allowing a total police state mentality to overwhelm us completely at home, with burgeoning military conquering nations abroad to boot.

Once while I was riding a Greyhound bus from Gainesville to Miami, Florida as a college student, I happened to sit next to a very bright and incisive English lady. We began to chat about different things in general, then suddenly began to compare my USA with her UK. The only thing that has stuck in my mind was her view that Americans have what she referred to as a *forced patriotism*. I shall never forget these two words the English lady uttered about my great land of the free. I was, of course, taken aback and felt a sense of insulting anger, yet managed not to overreact to her notions. At the time I thought she was way off base, yet as I matured the idea took hold and I could begin to see the idea more clearly, at least from her perspective.

Americans do appear to be forced or coerced to be patriotic by outwardly doing things that are rarely done in many other countries. The two things that came to her mind were flag-waving presentations and, most of all, the Pledge of Allegiance. The lady could not believe that school children recite the pledge everyday at the beginning of their school day. Even though nobody is *required* to do so, and some religious groups oppose its use, it is hard to deny that the whole process smacks of some sort of forced totalitarian credo.

Many people who travel to the USA immediately notice the proliferation of American flags on display here. Many business institutions proudly fly our flag in multiple displays with extremely large ones taking particular notice amongst the many smaller ones. Every public school classroom seems to be required to have one there as well. People have them affixed to their cars and homes to prove their personal loyalty to our government and its society. Could it be possible that Americans are worried that if they do not show some outward signs of American patriotism, that something bad might happen to them? It is just hard to believe that our proliferation of flag displays really makes much of a difference anyway, and appears to be more related to commercial profit than real love of country. The last bastion of a scoundrel is to hide behind the flag and its representation of patriotism.

Could we have most recently become a nation led by scoundrels, hiding behind our forced patriotism and flag? It is very possible that the scoundrels have actually tricked us into believing that their need to make war, along with the millions in blood money, are as American as mom and apple pie. I hope this is not actually the case, yet as I watch news returns about Iraq, I find it very difficult to think any other way.

The USA's civilian society is so connected to the military that it rewards military veterans with more points on an application for a job. What is a pacifist to do? Why should someone who has agreed to be in the military be considered any better than a religious person, unwilling to take up arms against another human being? It's the religious people and pacifists who have been at the forefront of our American foundations. Many of our original 13 British colonies which became states were founded as havens for various forms of religious denominations. Catholics, Puritans, Quakers, and Jews came to America to escape European religious persecution and the military there.

European immigrants were so anti-military on the whole that many came to America so their sons would not have to endure some country's draft system, in order to perpetuate the many useless wars of the various European Royal families during the 18th and 19th Centuries. The military draft was a dreaded system that swallowed up the European masses of the poor, in order to enrich the already absurdly wealthy. By coming to America, at least they had a chance to see their sons grow old, rather then being cut down in their prime.

The USA, at least, has almost completely done away with the draft system, as we last saw during the Vietnam War. However, Selective Service Registration is still the law of the land, even though it is not really fully implemented today as before. What has been substituted is a military system composed of volunteers, willing to put in their time for the express purpose of getting something back for their toil and trouble. Some men and women might even be serving out of patriotism, rather than dollars and cents. But if no war is available to fight, the idea behind serving one's country for unselfish reasons rapidly evaporates into thin air.

INVASION AND LOSS OF PRIVACY:

I can still remember my first Florida Driver's License. It was a green and white folding piece of paper with my name, address, date of birth, and other pertinent bits of information needed to distinguish me from other Floridians. But the one big thing it did *not* have on it in 1965 was my picture. The reason this was done was to avoid invading my privacy and in turn create some sort of a national ID card. Americans way back then could see what was coming and fought valiantly to delay the inevitable from taking away what nobody can ever give back to you once it's gone.

But little by little in the name of law and order, which is now called national security; our privacy has been eroded to the point of a tenuous nonexistence. Especially since the advent of computer databases and the like, we have become like a tadpole under the microscope in science class. Legally, American Constitutional purists balk at the idea of establishing a National ID card, but yet we skirt around the issue with databases full of information about us, including our prints and pictures. Just try to cash a check next time you go to the store without a picture of you on your driver's license and a credit card. You may as well be from Mars, because the Martian with proper ID will have a better chance than you.

Due to our technological advances in the cyber world in which we now live, our overly conservative Supreme Court has allowed itself to skirt the imbedded freedoms of our Federal Constitution. It knows that by doing so, it gradually increases the strength of the grip that our layers of government maintain to control their unwitting citizens. Little by little, the land of the free and the home of the brave is becoming the land of the controlled and the home of the apathetic. Once this process of connecting the *database dots* is complete, nobody will be free and certainly too scared to be brave anymore.

The USA has thousands of laws on the books that have sprung from all levels of government. From J-walking to pot-smoking laws, the government demands that you tow the line. The penalties for breaking the laws can range from a warning to death, depending upon the severity of the offense. However, with so many laws out here needing to be enforced, it's a wonder law enforcement personnel has any time to do anything but write reports and tickets.

But, just do not forget that anytime *the Man* wants to get you, he will find the place and the time. You'll be dead in the water, out of gas, up the creek, and in the slammer somewhere. When the powers that be are drastically challenged here today, just like in any other society whether past or present, the victim is likely to be YOU. So as the Buffalo Springfield song says; *get out of line, and the man will take you away.*

Remember, with so many laws on the books, it's likely you are probably breaking one right now. So it doesn't take much today for our omnipresent government to find a reason to put you away, or at least make your life very miserable, possibly forever. Everybody has a legal Achilles heel and every government, including ours, knows this. Their job is just made a lot easier today with all the convenient information at their hot little fingertips. Sometimes you may even get caught in the trap of entrapment by one police force or the other. Everybody who posts a website is fair game today. Cyber cops may try to offer you e-mail from fake kids, in order to see if you take the perverse-like bait. *Big Brother* in America is everywhere today, and the sooner we smell his coffee, the better chance we shall have to turn the tide of anti-privacy.

Americans need to be awake and aware of what is going on around them every moment, just to protect themselves from the chains of ignorance and complacency. Democracy works best with full time citizen participation and education. Totalitarian bliss is best served by an ignorant, complacent group of people. But because we are now so hard at work just to keep afloat, we really do not find the time to be on guard from the government encroachment on our privacy. With the standard of living appearing to be slipping through our tired, sleep-deprived hands, Americans could wake up tomorrow to find themselves living the true nightmare of George Orwell's book **1984.** The date may not jive, but the message is still the same.

Government in America must continue be the servant of its people, rather than the people the servants of their government masters. The Soviet Union collapsed for the very reason that people served the state. But don't think the USA is immune from the same totalitarian grip in the future if we are not a lot more cautious and questioning in general. From now on, your favorite word should be WHY? No switch is thrown and *poof,* you are no longer free. We allow the loss of freedom to happen to us bit by bit. People like Benjamin Franklin warned us to remain on guard in this respect, as freedom is not lost all at once, but rather gradually.

ARE WE OUT OF CONTROL?

It is very possible that many foreigners, as well as some Americans, may now feel or have even felt all along that American society is out of control. But what do I mean by the term "out of control"? What I mean is that too many strange and illegal things are going on for us to catch or stop. The laws of the land are either being deliberately circumvented or else completely ignored all together.

Let's begin with my favorite American black eye out of control immigration. Even with all the talk and news about poor economic immigrants sneaking into the United States to find dollars to send home, there are still others who somehow enter here who do not make it to the papers. The kind of people I am talking about are here with all the supposed legal papers in order, but with one major exception; everything they represented to our Embassies or immigration authorities is a sham.

I am talking about very dishonest people with connections and the necessary funds to beat the system and even prosper once they make it to our shores. Well-to-do criminals like drug cartels and assorted guerrilla organizations can easily "paper fool" almost any government official into thinking that they are the salt of the earth. As well, many of them can easily bribe Embassy and Consular officials abroad, where they are from, to rubber stamp their visa application. While abroad, I noticed that many of our Embassies and Consulates like to hire many third country nationals as well as citizens of the host country where the American Embassy is located. This is done to save money, have a reliable pool of low-level clerical talent available, and to facilitate language barriers. It is also done to not have too many Americans posted abroad, especially in dangerous nation-states such as Colombia or Saudi Arabia.

While in Riyadh, Saudi Arabia, I had many occasions to frequent our Embassy there in the Diplomatic Quarter. The time was a bit after the Gulf War in the early 1990's. The first thing I noticed was the high amount of non-American staff that worked there. For example, much of the security staff were Christians from Sri Lanka. They had Pakistani Muslims working as clerks behind the glass windows inside. They processed the visas that Saudi's presented in order to travel to the USA. However, many of the visas, as we later found out were not presented in person by the people requesting them. The Saudis hired local go-fers to stand in line to jump the hurdles presented by Embassy officials.

I can almost guarantee you that all the paperwork in Arabic presented to our Embassy was never even understood or ever verified as to its reality or truth. All I know is that if I had ever wanted a fake Marriage Certificate, stating I was married to whomever, that some Filipinos, with the blessing of a Saudi, could have gotten me one at any time. Many foreign nationals needed such fake paperwork to pretend they were married in Saudi Arabia, so they could be together in public legally with their girlfriends. It never mattered that they might both be married back home. Money talked, and any piece of paper walked out the back door.

It is too bad that matters such as 9/11 had to wake us up to these pressing realities that today still haunt us as a free nation. Remember that most of the terrorists aboard the jets that crashed into the World Trade Center Buildings were indeed from Saudi Arabia and most likely got their visas there with the help of corrupt clerks and go-fers.

Another example of this kind of paper trickery lies in the fact of our government's fear of allowing people to come here that are in any sort of possible economic necessity at home. Our government fears that somebody that has more to gain by coming here may not want to return to their Third World life in their own country. A middle-class clerk working in some hotel certainly has more to gain by getting into our dollar heaven than by going back to work for $200 per month back home. But what they do not seem to realize is that the middle class hotel clerk is probably a very honest, law-abiding citizen, who may love his home and family life more than the chance to make a lot of dollars and risk separation from loved ones.

Let's go one step further and assume the clerk decides to stay here illegally and work in the underground economy for cash. The chances are that the person will not break any laws while here and send home a lot of money to his family. His presence here will hardly be noticed, and he might even be able to get assistance to legalize his immigration status, as many millions have done already. It is more likely that this kind of immigrant can really help make our nation a better place to live at the end of the day. Even though he got here somehow under the fence, his motives and former life at home will make for an honest, hardworking person.

Now let's look at the other side of the coin: the immigrant with money, business at home, and no apparent reason to want to have to stay permanently in the USA. This is the kind of guy we should be looking at under an electron microscope very carefully. In this case scenario, our applicant usually applies for a tourist visa with some prearranged trip and goes with his family. He may even apply for a visa so he may enter many times for supposed business purposes.

Yes, it is true that our subject has lots of money or business back home, otherwise how could he afford a month with his wife and kids in Florida? But what we fail to investigate well is the history behind the money and/or business, the guy claims to have. Since any paperwork is easy to fake and money trails are not easy to follow abroad, it cold be very likely that our more qualified applicant is in reality a terrorist, a drug cartel member, or some sort of foreign mobster.

However, as long as the person looks good on paper, and that really means green and white paper, everything is supposed to be kosher. Mr. Big gets to go to Disney World with the wife and kids, while the middle-class, honest clerk gets stiffed by Uncle Sam. Our basis for immigration should not be solely based upon a person's apparent lack of need to stay in the USA, his apparent need to better his life economically; it should be based upon truth and the hope that the person desiring to come to America will make it a better place for all in which to live.

Heterogeneous American Population (the downside):

As I said before, sometimes your great strength can also be your weakness, if not moderated properly. The 17th Century Dutch philosopher Baruch Spinoza emphasized the need for humankind to *know its limitations.* That means that everybody can only go so far and for so long with their God-given talents and abilities. There will come a time when actions can begin to be actually counterproductive to oneself or his society in general.

Americans' great population of melting pot people has indeed led to our ability to get to the top of the heap internationally. But just because you are on top today is no guarantee that you really belong there in the first place or can remain there indefinitely. You see, it is because of our background, that outsiders such as the Europeans have viewed us throughout the years as a nation of criminal mongrels. American society looks like some sort of no-holds-barred free-for-all. To this day, there are actually some Europeans who are reticent or afraid to even visit the USA. They point to our cowboy/gun mentality first and foremost. This makes them feel unsure about venturing out of the lobby of an American international airport.

American movies have and continue to be made about violence related issues such as gangsters, cowboys vs. Indians, and present-day gang-related subcultures. Ask any European tourist if he has ever heard of Al Capone, and the answer is yes! But ask the same person something historical or cultural about his own backyard, and he might not know it. It goes to show you that our gangsters and violent society in general have made such a strong impact, that we are better known than anyone or anything abroad overall.

After WW1, my grandfather Reuben of Hamburg, Germany had a meeting around the kitchen table with his other brothers. They were all veterans of the German Army, defeated by the Allies in Europe. Germany was a broken country, with little hope in sight at the time. Inflation was out of control and prospects looked very dim for businessmen like them. They all really wanted to get the hell out of Germany and immigrate to some other country that had a bright future. The names of some underdeveloped and barely civilized nations popped up during the brainstorming session. South Africa, Brazil, and Palestine were at the top of the list in their order of consideration for emigration from Germany. One of the brothers mentioned the USA as a possibility, but the idea was soon abandoned rapidly, for the very reasons I have mentioned here regarding our unsavory reputation.

In the end, one brother went to Palestine, one went to Ecuador, while my grandfather stayed in Germany until 1933. As soon as Adolf Hitler came to power that same year, he fled to Belgium with his family. But by 1939 he, along with my Uncle Werner and Grandmother Fannie were all dead, as the Germans marched into Antwerp and occupied my family's stately home. Thank God my uncle Manfred and my father Sig managed to evade the Nazi capture, eventually making it to the so called *violent shores of America*. Those sometimes anti-Semitic shores were not easy to penetrate then, but somehow they made it, and each raised their families in New York City and Miami.

Today, "anything *almost* goes" seems to be the catch phrase. We are free, but where are our limits in good judgment and good taste, or even moral and religious values upon which our forefathers based this country? I, in no way, could ever be construed as some prude or religious fanatic, because I have seen the plank in my own eye. I am able to smell my own shit clearly and it does stink, too. I will even go so far as to admit that I am a jerk to boot. But even I, a 53 year old ex-wild man of the 60's and 70's, am alarmed by what I see today in the USA.

Much of the problem lies in what I refer to as a dilution of each of America's distinct culture and customs. We have become so homogenized now that it could be said to be causing a lack of identity in clear, unblurred cultural and social pathways of our youth to follow. Depending upon one's ethnic background lays the path for them to follow socially, culturally, and possibly even religiously. American youth is now following a sort of mixed-up, trendy social scene they get from assorted media and the assorted music cultures they learn about daily. Whatever is *in* now is taken for face value and has become their cultural pathways of enlightenment. There appears to be no real deep-rooted understanding of the whole process for them. But because so much money and glamour is associated with it, mainstream America goes for it <u>ad nauseum</u>.

The first time I ever confronted this phenomenon of cultural dilution, along with the cross-cultural imitation that ensues, was when I did my ROTC summer training at Ft. Bragg, NC. We called it Fayettnam, because it took place in Fayetteville, where the Army post is located. The year happened to be 1970, when the useless, yet tragic Viet Conflict was still in its full-blown glory. One of the African-American cadets who was very gung-ho got the name OREO. The poor guy really felt terrible because I, along with some of the other cadets, gave him that handle. But, we couldn't stand to see what the US Army was doing to him spiritually and ethnically. The guy was very black, yet he began to talk and act whiter than even a pure Honkey like me. The other African-American cadets really got under his skin the most, but when some of the white guys could even see the same phenomenon, too, he really began to flip out.

The cadet we called OREO was black on the outside, yet white on the inside, just like the cookie produced by Nabisco. What was coming through to everyone was not the man's black culture, but a soft-white frosty version of himself. It wasn't real, and nobody bought it for one minute. The guy finally came up to me with a timid explanation of why he was acting so white. He confided to me that he was the first member of his family to have the chance at becoming an Army Officer. His other older male family members seem to have served or been serving as enlisted men, making it up to the ranks. My co-cadet pathetically thought that by imitating someone else's culture, he would have a better chance of getting to the finish line to make his family proud.

I can appreciate the cadet's motives, but that does not make it agreeable to my psyche or to my perception of what is dictated by common sense. I am sure that the other black cadets made it just fine and that nobody failed them because they were too black for the Army. Nowadays, we have a reverse of the OREO phenomenon. American white and Hispanic youth are trying to imitate black culture, and in most cases they are not even imitating the positive aspects of the African-American culture. What our youth appear to be taking from the African-American culture is the negative, violent and *ghettoesque* version of the troubled poorer members of American society.

This social phenomenon is not unique to us, but to countries everywhere. The first time I came across a real cross cultural imitation bonanza was in Miami. I saw a young man that appeared to be black, maybe Jamaican. But as I got closer, I realized the guy was neither really black nor Jamaican by any stretch of the imagination. What we had that day was a young Japanese fellow, who had just returned from a long vacation in Jamaica. He was dressed in a Jamaican reggae-style get-up and his hair was all done in dreadlocks. Later, I found out that Jamaica was a very popular vacation destination for Japanese youth. It is the kind of place where the Japanese can detach from their rigid culture at home and literally let their hair down.

I can't say this kind of cultural imitation was permanent or even harmful to anyone, yet it does show the lengths that people will go to in order to feel better about themselves. But to me the bottom line should be that people are in touch with who they really are and where they come from. Trans-cultural tripping might not be the path to find happiness, because in the end no one can run away from themselves or their true cultural identity.

In America, we have every possible combination of social, ethnic, and economic groups. People of varied backgrounds have been getting married to each other for years and have produced offspring of such a mixed bloodline, that in the end very few Americans really know for sure where they came from with any certainty. A lot of Americans who thought they were all white, have found, out to their dismay, that they were actually descendants of African-American families. The converse also holds true, as African Americans have discovered their white roots.

This multicultural cocktail assures us that when it comes to the question of intelligence or abilities, that it would be pure folly to stereotype any American based upon his exterior makeup. Anybody in America can be qualified as either a jerk or a stupid ass. No one group holds a monopoly on these two categories in which I have lumped the negative, insensitive, and mean members of our own fragile humanity. After all, most people have average intelligence, some are below average, and even fewer are above average. People with a genius-level intelligence are the rarest. But, intelligence levels alone do not guarantee that the person doesn't fall into one of the two categories. As a matter of fact, we all exhibit many aspects of either one of the two groups from time to time. Certainly you can remember a time when you did something you regretted later. You probably felt like an ass or a jerk. When you begin to analyze yourself and those around you, ask yourself or your friend in which of the two categories they fall.

If somebody takes offense to this categorization technique that usually means they think neither of the two applies to them. Be very wary of this kind of person, because in the end they shall betray you or even try to hurt you. My simple suggestion is that when you meet a person for the first time, try to figure out in which group you and they fall. Go so far as to **ask them** if they are a jerk or an ass, just to view their reaction and make sure to try and explain something about the two categories of humanity. Tell the other person up front that **you** are either a jerk or a stupid ass. But remember that when a person thinks of themselves too highly you should remind them that *nobody is perfect.* At the end of the day it doesn't matter in which category a person falls, because everything is relative depending upon personality, intelligence, and present circumstances. You or I could be put in either one of the two groups at anytime by anyone able to make that decision.

I don't want anyone to think that I go around judging people all day, nor should you. Having a judgmental attitude about people is something which creates a negative and ungodly attitude. It is something to be avoided at all cost. However, the idea of putting people in two imperfect states of consciousness allows everyone to see the folly of thinking that their shit doesn't stink, or that they are any better or smarter than anyone else in the eyes of God.

To me, everybody is at the same level whenever I meet them. I could care less about their station in life ... I treat a president the same way I treat a maid because we are all just flesh and blood. It's only after our interaction do I begin to either think less or more of them. I can decide my feelings about people as time goes by and our level of contact increases. Just because somebody is your boss does not give them the right to treat you like shit all day. People need to treat each other with respect. Do you remember the golden rule? It comes from the Talmud and reminds us to treat others the way we want to be treated ourselves. "Do unto others as you would have them do unto you." This simple piece of advice is so forgotten and overlooked in America today that it has created epidemic proportions of modern American jerks and ass.

It's nice to be important, but it's more important to be nice. This credo should be next to *In God We Trust* on our money to remind everyone in the USA that God alone isn't going to solve all our problems everyday. This leads me to how lousy we are currently treating our children who are our future, after all. What we have now are highly intelligent youth with low social skills and a poor education. Our school systems are generally failing the future of our nation at every turn. But what the adults responsible for them fail to realize is that their benign neglect is also causing a kind of unspoken despondency among our children.

When people become despondent, they feel like losers. They tend to act out in negative ways that run counterproductive to the goals of a healthy society. When a kid has nothing to do, no place to play and bored stiff, frustration will surely ensue. Yes, we do have many parks, but too many times they are locked up and the kids can't get in to play and relax. We need more parks and other green spaces in the urban areas for everyone, not just young people. But all too often, developers, in collusion with their political friends, who make the rules, allow this necessary aspect so needed in our country to be conveniently overlooked. Every square foot of available land is used to build on, while the green spaces get obliterated forever. The world turns into some sort of ghetto: one for the rich and another for the poor.

The easiest example I can give on this matter is by looking at public school yards. These areas of green, space or even paved over open space for school children, are fast disappearing. School yards are now constantly replaced by prefabricated classrooms that are portable in nature. The kids are winding up with practically no place for them to run free, play, or exercise in a proper manner. Rather than coughing up the money for new schools, the adults of America have allowed older schools to go to the dogs, along with the kids attending them. What we have left are sick schools, sick teachers, sick kids, and a politically sick social system based upon corruption, greed, cronyism, and incompetence.

Schools systems the nation over are all paying the price for too many years of buck-passing and no real planning. We refuse to put up the crosswalk lights until some kid gets hit by a car on the way to school … Is it really necessary to wait until somebody has to die before common sense prevails? Our children suffer from obesity more than ever, because they are crammed into portable classrooms staring at some computer with no place to run around.

New modern schools are windowless to save on construction and energy costs. This supposedly also makes kids focus more on their studies because they get less distracted from looking out the windows. However, this mentality breaks the spirit of kids by disallowing them to daydream, use their vivid imagination, or just detach for a couple of minutes from whatever the class may be doing at the time. Studies have been made linking daydreaming to positive aspects necessary for a healthy mind and learning environment.

It is no wonder parents are yanking their children out of these education sweatshop factories and deciding on home schooling as a remedy. As it is turning out, home-schooled kids do just as well and in many instances, much better academically. At the recent spelling bee national finals there was a very high percentage of home-schooled kids, though statistically their numbers are far fewer in relation to mainstream education. For some reason Americans always have the money for bombs and bullets. We always seem to be able to find some place to invade or liberate depending upon one's point of view. That's why teachers are now forced to dig into their own meager pockets in order to buy school supplies for students.

One thing that it appears that most of the colonizers of the New World did was to wipe out the Indians, or the indigenous peoples of the Americas. The new Americans followed exactly in their footsteps and continued the path of death by disease, slavery, starvation, massacre, and, finally, through good old assimilation (American style.) I once took some Spaniards on a tour of an Indian village near Miami because they had never seen a real live Indian before. To my amazement, they were still very much guilt-ridden from their country's days of colonial despotism and butchery of the Indian population in America.

It was kind of like the same reaction you might expect from a German after he viewed a concentration camp in Europe. My point is that no matter how proud we are as Americans today, we must never forget the way we treated the non-Europeans we came into contact with on this continent. European-Americas also took away the drums from the African slaves brought over to work like dogs. Europeans knew that this lack of the tribal unity, spirit, and African power would almost surely break the back of any chance for unity that might have been used against the masters.

Assimilation of non-European peoples was also marked by name changes where slaves took the names of their masters. Christianity was also forced upon them as well, therefore eradicating tribal and animistic religions or traditions. African-American men were forced to sublimate their masculine prowess, thereby causing the rise of a matriarchal society. This led to poor role models for children, little paternal responsibility, and a weak support system financially for the family unit overall. We pay the price daily in America even today due to these historical times of shame and unbearable wrongs.

Today's America is marked by an ever increasing rate in illegitimate children of all races, children who are being raised by their grandmothers and grandfathers, that is, if they are lucky. Otherwise, they can be thrown into some foster care system, where foster parents seek state money and wind up making a business of the whole process. I have even heard rumors of state foster care supervisors demanding kickbacks from the very foster families they O.K. placement for. After all, everybody has their hand out today, from rip-off multinationals like Enron or MCI WorldCom, to the array of beggars on our crowded streets.

The very backbone of any country is the family unit. But today, the states have gotten directly involved in deciding what is good or bad for our family structure. The family is a sacred bond of blood and laws that our government daily encroaches upon. By weakening the family bonds, it in essence strengthens itself to eventually become our total master. Our autonomy as individuals and unique groups of people becomes broken, just as our families are being broken up today.

America is full of runaway children, most of them from foster care nightmare situations forced upon them by under-funded state agencies and courts. The left hand many times never knows what the right hand is doing, so we find ourselves with dead or missing children victims all legally sanctioned by government. When the state has the power to take a child from its family, it has the power of life and death over the future of all families in America.

Supposedly, the wish of the state is for the welfare and safety of the children that it vows to protect. However, the structures are never in place most of the time for the removed child to really depend on until they become adults. Since governments in the USA have managed to take on almost every conceivable role in our modern society, the agencies in question have become overburdened with work. They simply have bitten off more than they could ever chew.

You might imagine that such pressing matters as family and child safety programs would be properly funded, just as public education should be properly funded. But the buck stopped somewhere in the smoke-filled back room of a slimy politician in a state capital or in Washington DC. The money is never there because it is never appropriated in the first place. How much more must the middle class pay in taxes before there is no more middle class? Since they pay the lion's share of taxes, anyway, we can't expect more help from the people living from paycheck to paycheck.

We therefore must turn to corporate America and the multinationals so deeply involved in the military-industrial complex. But these guys never want to pay for our problems and laundry list of mistakes throughout history. So they buy politicos in order to pass tax legislation that legally allows them to escape their moral and ethical responsibilities forever. It's called lobbying, or legalized bribery, American-style. Next time you observe any political race, just look to see how much is spent and who gives how much to whom. I can guarantee you that the big winners always suck up to the multinational corporations, because they know they can get the best cost benefit ratio from these amoral worldwide institutions of never-ending expansion and control. A perfect example of this domination and control issue is the great multinational General Electric Company or GE as most know it.

Whenever you watch NBC Nightly News programs, remember that the parent company of NBC is the great GE. If you go forward to connect the dots, then you shall realize the great influence the powerful players of our military-industrial complex have on our opinion shaping-processes. I don't think you'll ever hear a story on NBC about the role of GE in Iraq or Saudi Arabia in the world today. Yet they are always there or in other corners of the world, like Texas-based Bechtel Corporation, enabling American-sanctioned dictators and despots to remain in power; that is until our government and its hoard of companies no longer has any use for them.

SELF-WORTH IN AMERICA

In the United States, one's self-worth is generally measured only by the size of their bank account. If a person has a lot of money, he then feels pleased by himself, while the people he is trying to associate with look at that person in awe. The word "successful" attaches itself to that person, and the magic of the money makes that person more worth to society than a person of little means.

If you ask most kids what they want to be when they grow up, they always say some occupation that can earn them a lot of money, once they realize the dollar value associated with each job. Their parents and friends indirectly coax them to go for the gold. It is hard to go in other directions where money is not so great an enticement.

Americans also have an unrealistic fear of losing what they have, because that would mean a loss of self-worth and status in society. Some people who lose professional positions in America would rather use up their savings first, and then take a job beneath their social station. There have been cases of suicide related to such situations. Such drastic measures were not necessary, had the individual not measured their self-worth by the job they perform. If they could have only taken any honest position, then gone on from there to improve the status of their predicament, such horrors would not have occurred.

Today, most Americans fear helping others to better themselves, partially because they think that they might lose something they have to the person being helped. Help is very restrained in America now and never fully given with a clear conscience. For this reason, a permanent underclass of poor has been created. An example of this is our veterans from Viet Nam, not being properly taken care of since they got home. The cycle of war, the street, and homelessness is in our face every day we drive to any major urban center in our country.

TOO INTELLIGENT?

Can anyone actually be categorized as too intelligent? Well, sure they can. Just ask people who apply for jobs that are constantly being screened out with phrases like "overqualified for the position". One man was turned down for a job as a police officer in a New England state because his entrance exam score on the IQ portion was too high. It seems as though people with high intelligence are allowed to work in positions only for very specific task-oriented situations in government or industry. However, they are not needed for actual jobs that require real thinking or imagination. It's IQ too high and say good-bye.

Rod Serling's "Twilight Zone" once had an episode where two parents feared some test that their young son had to take by government decree when he reached a certain age. However, their fears were based upon their son scoring too high, rather than too low. It appears that this futuristic society eliminated children who were categorized too intelligent, for fear of upsetting the status quo engineered by their government and society.

Our nation glorifies the police, military, and other government service occupations as well, yet by choice it deliberately eliminates the best and brightest from service. Just remember that the first group of policemen ever sanctioned by government was in London, England. The government recruited street thugs and ruffians to fill the ranks and paid them to patrol the streets and keep order. Have we really made any progress in this regard? Are we allowing people to protect us who have underlying tendencies to be bullies and thickheaded thugs? My answer to this question is "yes". Sociopaths and bullies are in uniforms all over America and their mental skills are unfortunately not as good as they could be.

In 2020 this is still wingnate, almost psycho

PUBLIC TRANSPORTATION

Before the mass production of automobiles in the late 19th Century, America was slowly, but surely developing mass transportation in its cities and rural areas, in the form of street cars, trolleys, and trains. However, once Henry Ford figured out a way to enable everyone to afford a car, it seems to have doomed us to a life of asphalt-paved highways covered by cars and trucks. This led to the inherently free spirited American to throw caution to the wind, abandoning reason for passion (public transportation for the automobile).

Most of the United States of America has nonexistent or poor-quality public transportation, except in the richer and more affluent cosmopolitan areas of our nation such as New York, Chicago, or San Francisco. Most of the public relies on buses to get around, a direct off-shoot of the car and its internal combustion engine. Our nation's train system is very backward and sometimes even dangerous (crashes and derailments). The train system is mostly used to haul freight, with little regard for passenger traffic. Both freight and passenger traffic is underutilized, as we rely too heavily on inefficient cars and giant trucks.

Our formerly beautiful pristine countryside, now paved over everywhere, is a series of interconnected clogged and congested roads and highways. They have created most of our air pollution, which has led to increased global warming from the greenhouse effect. Our nation's kids are being forced to play in parking lots rather than parks, as green space for parks and recreation has made way for urban sprawl.

The independent spirit of Americans seems to be our Achilles heel, too. The desire for our "self-transportation" society has also led to mass death and destruction, caused by unsafe 'do it yourself' driving. Since not everyone's state of driver readiness can be monitored 24/7, no matter how hard big brother government tries, this massacre of around 50,000 per year shall continue. Our desire to form a more perfect union, at least in this scenario, comes unraveled. Yet since the industry associated with free-spirited transportation is our nation's largest cash cow, it is ever unlikely the madness will ever completely stop. Just stop and think how many businesses revolve around the auto industry, and you can see how a complete overhaul of our way of life could be at stake the cars should run out of gas someday. Empires could even crumble while the strong weaken.

Self-transportation also changes our personalities by the isolationist effect it has upon us. It perpetuates egotism, an uncaring numbing of the senses, as well as an innate fear and insecurity overall. People who drive themselves everyday lose their spontaneous desire to socialize with strange people, therefore losing the ability to trust others. Public transportation not only is safer and more efficient than cars, it also lets us meet and interact with others they might meet on a bus or a train.

Airplane travel also has the same effect, as we are forced to sit down with a seat belt, unable to move around and meet other passengers. Air travel is now even more dangerous as made by the threat of terrorism and hijacking. Overall, our trust level is at an all-time low, and it is partially caused by our free spirited need to do it ourselves alone.

TRUST IS A THING OF THE PAST

As our isolation on a daily basis increased, trust also seems to have gone by the wayside. Any grandmother with big boobs is a likely suspect at the airport. After all, she could be carrying dope or a boob bomb! Why are you smiling and being so friendly in the first place? Maybe it's because you are really a crook or a terrorist in disguise.

But trust, after all is what built our nation and its great government throughout the centuries. Things used to be done or sealed by a simple handshake. Our trust level is constantly being diminished daily. Once the trust goes, so does our democratic society, along with its vibrant capitalist economy. The US dollar is only as strong as the trust we have in ourselves, our leaders, and our government. Take away the trust, and the whole system falls apart overnight.

MAKE TOMORROW LIKE TODAY!

Americans have gotten too used to the same way of doing things for too long a time. Our society has become sedentary and lazy. People are becoming obese at an alarming rate, as the fat people now rule the world. What we are trying to do is make a comfort zone based upon what works for us today, and let it be the guide for tomorrow, even though it may not be the best path for us to follow. We think inside the box that we have built to isolate us from the world's realities.

Thank God America has never really suffered to the same extent as many other nations, though we have had our share of terrible experiences including, but not limited to, the following: starvation, genocide, war, ethnic discrimination, racism, religious intolerance, corruption, and social indifference by our governmental entities. But by today's standards, the average American has never actually walked in the moccasins of, for example, the Native American, as he was forced into the Oklahoma Territory so long ago.

When the nations of white European farmers invaded America to colonize, they came into sharp contrast and immediate conflict with tribes of indigenous hunters. It was a battle and then war of farmers against hunters. Due to the fact that a society of farmers is better organized and able to stand and keep its ground, the tribes of hunter nations could not compete for long with the more advanced technology of farmer peoples.

The Indians may have lost the battles, but America lost the war in the long run. Just look around and see carbon copy cities all over the United States of America. The modern equivalent of American farmers have found themselves unable to hunt for new experiences in life and, as stated before, made us lead a very sedentary and overly regimented life style; this is in part due to our over-reliance on military techniques used in the past to fight Indians and invade other nations as well, General Custer excluded.

We have nothing to fear now but the rampant boredom our lives have to experience daily. You know: the same routine of work, work, more work, and then home to do some more. We are so busy looking inward that we are unable to literally or figuratively hunt for game or new rewarding life experiences. We now get our kicks on Route 66, meaning cars, drugs, booze, mindless sex, and video related boob tubes like TV or cyber space. Talking to or meeting with a neighbor for a cup of coffee is absolutely out of the question for now.

Our Native Americans, whom we had so much disdain for, tried to teach us another way of life, but it was already too late by the time our ancestors got to the shores of the Americas. The great self-reliant tribes of hunters were asked to leave the party, and if they didn't go, they were simply driven out or massacred. Free spirits have now been replaced by predictably insecure, untrusting hoards of over-weight people.

THE WORLD'S LARGEST ECONOMY

Most people don't quite realize it, but the fact is that the United States economic system is responsible for the production of a tad over 40% of the worlds' goods and services. This means that everybody else combined produce the other 57 to 60 percent. Japan, then Germany, are next in the economic pecking order, but together they make up about only 30 % of the world's goods and services. After these three countries are through calling the shots, what is ever left over is allowed to be produced and/or consumed by everybody else. It really means that the rest of the world pie is not big enough to adequately feed, clothe, and house the billions of others sharing the planet. This is not really fair, but, then again, life is for some reason not fair anyway.

Simply because life is not fair, it doesn't mean that mankind, or especially Americans, should be apathetic to the world's needs, and especially to the needs of our fellow Americans so great in need themselves. This leads us to the modern day 21st Century phenomenon we can call *standard of living slippage.* We are now seeing great increases in poverty at home as the overall standard of living erodes daily. Today it takes two wage earners to sustain the homes that were once sustained by a sea of single wage earners.

Everybody has to work in order to live as more income gets taxed and spent by the multitude of governments and their-ever increasing bureaucracies. The result has forced government to step in to find a remedy for the situation of latchkey kids, devoid of any parental supervision almost all day long. Who is minding the kids if everybody is outside working just to survive? Ozzie and Harriet didn't need daycare for Ricky and David because Harriet got to stay home and be a fulltime mom.

Teachers know the problem of out-of-control kids and families only too well. Most kids still have both their parents at home at the primary school level, but by the time they reach secondary school, the divorces and the associated problems occur. It's very hard to keep it all together as a family when so many factors based upon two wage earners' survival eat away at its structural foundations. If mom comes home from work, too tired to cook, most dads don't want to hear it, and the stress levels just skyrocket.

America needs stable, safe, and affordable daycare. Yet when a small city like Miami Springs tried to accomplish this, they were told to take a hike by the city's churches and private providers. The City charged much less, so the politics of survival forced them to stop offering the daycare services, so greatly needed by the blue-collar working moms and dads of the area. Tell me how we expect mom to work if she can't even find an affordable place to leave her kids during the day.

THE AMERICAN DIET

The American diet is overly rich in carbohydrates, sugars, and fats, making us the most obese nation on the face of the Earth. We also in turn are getting lazier by the minute, but with the added negative trait of also being hyperactive in the process.

This strange combination of contrary factors has led to our children and many adults to become unable to focus on what they need to do, in order to get through their day successfully. Kids are too lazy to study and can't focus on reading, which requires a longer attention span. They have more emotional outbursts, temper tantrums, and socialization problems in the process. American adults basically carry these kinds of underlying factors into the workplace, but are better able to mask them from years of learning to cover-up and play the system's inherent rules of self-preservation. However, their personal at home problems usually surface at work and eventually cause great economic loss and turmoil in the workplace.

Our diet and food, laden with added hormones, chemicals, and genetically enhanced substances, have got us against the ropes. We are still standing, but we are getting pounded in the head and guts at the same time. We can't keep playing rope-a-dope forever, as the constant pummeling from bad diet and dangerous food substances will eventually make us fall to the canvas in a stupor. All the children and adults in America with ADHD (attention deficit hyperactivity disorder) get even more hyperactive as they lose their ability to focus almost completely that is without chemical medicines, usually amphetamines. But if they were to change their diet to include more omega 3 fatty acids, for example, it could help them to improve in a shorter period of time.

I have been taking fish oil and flax seed oil for about a year and have noticed marked improvement in my peace of mind and ability to focus better mentally on the tasks at hand. Recent studies with inmates have also proven positive results as far as behavior is concerned. Our modern diet is lacking in these nutrients that coat our brain. Without enough Omega 3 fatty acids in our system, we cannot function at a level of peak efficiency.

BETTER SCREENING

Our public servants, such as policemen and detectives, need to be screened for signs of ADHD before they are given free reign to pound their beats or investigate people's lives. Their diet and eating habits should also be viewed. However, today the only real concern is screening for drugs and a criminal past. Just because someone has no record or doesn't use cocaine and heroin doesn't mean they are qualified.

A person with ADHD and a diet poor in Omega fatty acids could be an aggressive personality, tending to bully others once finding himself in a position of authority. I can't see how a hard-drinking, donut-chomping, non-degreed police officer, with an itchy trigger finger, can do us any good. Yet look around, and you will see just that in many police forces across the nation. The biological dysfunction of a person cannot be measured on a psychological test to screen out bullies from a police force.

More intensive medical forms of testing must be instituted before people are allowed to walk the walk and talk the talk of policemen. Our public safety is at stake, as well as the overall ability of crime solving. Crime will continue to pay for the white and blue collar types as long as the unqualified try to catch and convict the professional high functioning criminal personality types. Giving a cop a bullet proof vest and a nice Glock won't do the job alone. The brain ultimately is the answer to crime fighting, so only the best should be allowed to participate in the quest at crime fighting.

PERMANENT UNDERCLASS

To date, the Americas has had legalized slavery and/or indentured servitude in its midst longer than it hasn't. Slavery in the USA existed until the Civil War of the 1860's and even longer in Brazil up until the beginning of the 20th Century, when it was still ruled by emperors. It may not be technically legal in the 21st Century; however, it readily exists in our backyards today.

If we leave the big cities and travel into the poor rural areas of America, especially in agricultural areas, there is where we find the actual vestiges of cruelty and exploitation so long associated with slavery. Do we dare ask how the food gets on our tables? Was it produced by some poor non-English speaking person, smuggled into our nation? If it was, then does that person have to try and pay off unpayable debts until he can return home once again? Yes, I answer you my *perfect Americans*; it is very possible.

The chain of events doesn't stop there, however. Because even a 'nobody' of a farm worker needs love once in a while, that is if he has any money left over. So, he hooks up with a pretty female, possibly from the same place back home, and has his way with her for a few minutes. Paying the $21, 20 for the girl and $1 for the condom, is repeated over and over as more and more men stand in line outside the trailers. So, we now see that sexual slavery exists as well, alongside the conventional indentured servitude for the others. *Find out*

Of course, not everybody who enters our borders illegally winds up like a slave, or worse, even dead. Others go to the big cities and work in illegal sweat shops, knocking out fancy garments to be sold only at the best stores. At the end of the day, most of these illegally exploited immigrants wind up staying here simply because our government does not have the resources or real desire to deport them. The proverbial blind eye always comes in real handy, since these poor people are paid next to nothing. The underclass helps the big guys keep their labor costs extremely low, and don't forget that there is also the added benefit of no unions. *Underclass helps the employer make more $*

After years of sweating it out in the USA, some go on to jump through the hoops long and well enough to apply for American citizenship. Depending upon the examiner and their mastery of the simple rudiments of English questions

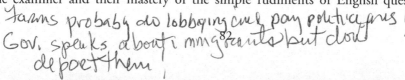

Farms probably do lobbying and pay politicians! Gov. speaks about immigrants but don't deport them!

must one Speak Eng to be an american citizen?

required for the citizenship exam, the multitudes of non-English speaking peoples go on to hold American citizenship. Those who wait long enough to become citizens are even exempted for the English requirements due to their advanced age.

What has been created by years of greed, exploitation, and good old governmental benign neglect is a permanent non-English speaking underclass of poor undereducated, *un-American-like Americans*. It may walk like a duck or look like a duck, but if it doesn't quack like one, then it's not a duck! *Are gringos the enemy?*

The new breed of Americans are easy prey for greasy politicians who pander to their ethnic fears as they paint the Gringos (for example) as the enemy. When you don't speak or understand English very well, it's easy to be bamboozled into thinking that Uncle Sam is always out to get you, so you vote for the guy speaking your language promising to protect you.

The living standard of the *look alike Americans* is on the average, lower than the national average and for a good reason. The premeditated cycle of low incomes allows for a population of eager or even desperate low paid labor. As Miami, Florida has become the poorest major metropolitan city in the USA, overflowing with non-English speaking legal and nonlegal people, the city has had to pay the price. High crime, low pay with no overtime pay, few good jobs, overcrowded dangerous schools, hospitals, roads, courts, jails, and, of course, legions of corrupt cops, judges, lawyers, politicians, civil servants, and bureau- *Wow!* crats. It has gotten so bad in Miami that even cabbies must pay bribes to hotel bell men, valet parking attendants, rental car agents, and the like, just to get a decent fare to the airport or beyond. The same kind of people that drive the cabs are demanding the bribes and you can be assured they are mostly recently arrived immigrants, forced to back stab their own kind to get ahead. Old habits and ancient customs die hard even in the USA when brought here from their home countries, where the mess is even worse than here. But some of our home-grown Americans despicably jump on the bandwagon embracing the corruption wholeheartedly, perhaps going on to even surpass their immigrant cohorts and coworkers. Allowing the permanent underclass to grow and continue to thrive should *Right* not be encouraged by Americans. All it leads to is a permanent lowering of the working and living standards for most of us, excluding the few lucky ones at the top of the economic pyramid. Eventually, the fat cats feel the pinch, too, when we suffer an economic recession or depression. Just remember; that the average guys in America are the largest group overall. If they can't buy things on a regular basis, the economy as a whole goes into a serious tailspin. Stocks plummet, banks close, and economic pandemonium ensues as fortunes on paper are all lost over-

Right!

night. The *modern indentured servants,* hooked on easy credit, just jump out of the windows or declare bankruptcy as is the case now, in record numbers.

We are

The 99% are more modern indentured servants

WOMEN IN AMERICA

It is unfortunate that American women are not getting paid what they are worth today in the workplace. It is even more tragic that after being indirectly forced out the front door of their homes to look for work with the men-folk, American women lag far behind in almost all areas of gainful employment.

Yes, every woman should be able to have a job or career if they decide to; however, it appears that all the sacrifice to study, work, and advance socially and economically is not really worth all the effort in the end.

Even though women make up a little over half the population, they earn far less than their male counterparts. Adding fuel to the female fires of injustice is their demanding home life, which still includes lots of cooking, cleaning, and child rearing. Men still basically depend upon the ladies to do the chores at home and bring home part of the bacon, too. These added demands have caused the American women to get overly stresses and burned out in the process. Men in turn also pay for the ladies' big schedules by feeling the brunt of their pain and anguish on a daily basis. Divorce rates have skyrocketed since the days of Ozzie and Harriet, while kids wander around the Internet or streets unsupervised to get into whatever mischief that awaits.

Getting out into the workplace isn't all it's cracked up to be, as the American women have taken on the ill-mannered mores of their male counterparts. Women are now seen as sluts around the world because they are portrayed by the media as able and willing partners of one-night stands. Yes, American women have gotten their freedom, but at the cost of becoming confused as to their goal of ultimate happiness. The mental units of hospitals across the nation are full of women in their thirties and forties, ready to commit suicide after having suffered through a series of sexually charged relationships, where the illusions of Prince Charming have never materialized.

The feminine needs of true love, a stable home, and family have been dashed upon the rocks of the marketplace. The accomplishments American women have made can not be taken for granted, but the cost to our family unit and female integrity has been very high in the process. Have women accomplished the goal of self-actualization, or have they actually adopted an imaginary penis in order to further compete with men in the workplace and now bedroom/boardroom? Have women become so sexually open that they risk exposing themselves to degrading their status as wife, mother, future nurturers, and caretakers of our social framework?

But, it's just as much the fault of the American men in their desire for seeing sex as nothing more than a physical exercise to exchange bodily fluids. (Men do not get attached as emotionally when engaging in sex as women do.) Women desire love and caring to go along with the physical portion much more so than the men. It must be in the best interests of the men to be careful not to harm the great givers of life.

Women can gain a new freedom from working outside the home, but if they do, the establishment that requires their services at a much reduced rate should make their transition smoother, by allowing them to tend to home and family whenever necessary. But the contrary remains. Women are not allowed to take much if any time off, without serious repercussions occurring to their job stability (Women are caught between a rock and a hard place: family or economic survival. If a woman is pressured too much, even her survival is at stake once the overdose happens. Then the family is really shattered, and no amount of money in the world can ever make it whole again.

FARMING OUT OUR WORK

It wasn't too long ago that almost everything Americans bought at the store was made in America. The imported goods were usually of poorer quality than their American counterpart. Everybody bought American! Imported goods were usually cheaply made things with low prices from the Far East. European goods like cars and radios were a step better than their Asian competitors, but in the end no match for our homemade products. We made and sold everything to ourselves and to the rest of the world.

Once on a trip to Lima, Peru in the mid 1960's, I was asked if I wanted to sell some wealthy Peruvians my American made shirts, which at the time I was wearing! The quality and style was so good that people would actually try to buy the shirt off your back overseas. Things we took for granted were valued prizes in other nations. Everything we did or even wore, represented American greatness, as our workhorse making widgets or Jets, made us all look and feel special.

Americans were almost fully employed for years after WW2, as their guts, know-how, and fly-by-the-seat-of-your-pants attitude helped us to gain market shares, unseen by any nation on Earth previously. By 1969, we had reached the Moon; no nation could touch us! Today we have high unemployment and one recession after another, except around election time every four years or so. People over 40 are disposable and being recycled in the job market only when the youngster supply is exhausted.

The questions then begs for answers: what has happened to the once great American society? Why is almost everything we now buy being made somewhere else? Are the millions of homeless people here to stay? Yes, if we continue to bury our heads in the sand (sand is still American the last time I looked). But sand is one of the few things left not being imported, yet!

Since the end of WW2, the formerly all-American companies have now joined hands with overseas investors, to create what we refer to as the multinationals. These Goliaths of business and industry now rule the planet not only financially, but politically as well. Their tentacles are in every possible facet of our lives, from toothpaste to nuclear bombs. So it makes perfect financial sense that when you have a cheaper place outside the USA, to set up shop there. Shipping the goods home still comes out better in the end, than having to make those widgets at home.

We refer to this process or phenomenon as *farming out the work* to others. It's not a pretty process from start to finish, but today it appears to be the way business and politics are conducted. It basically works like this;

1. Laws are passed to facilitate the business relocation and importation of the goods

2. Legally operating lobbyists grease politicians' hands in ways not even the most corrupt banana republic politico could ever dream of to assure continued cooperation and collaboration.

3. Cheaper made foreign good are allowed to flood our market place, thereby driving American competitors either completely out of business, or looking for some safe haven overseas to compete on the same level.

Unfortunately, the latter part of section 3 is what drives our companies today: the relocation to some economic safe haven. This is where sweat shops, greed, and exploitation are the order of the day. Right now, I am wearing a pair of sexy black American label, shorts which my wife bought for me at Sam's Club in Miami. However, their place of production is Kenya, Africa. Are Americans too dumb now even to make a stinking pair of shorts? I don't think so! But, if we did make the shorts here, we'd go out of business real fast. So why bother to go to the trouble, when the playing field is not level anymore?

Killing jobs at home has its related social consequences in the form of drug or alcohol abuse, mental illness, and family disintegration. Men who have no hope can get messed-up pretty quickly with the aforementioned three big societal evils. Remember that the people who spend the most and also pay the most taxes are the same poor class of people now out of work due to the farming-out strategies of corporate board rooms. The economic engine that drives the whole world are the same people now on the verge of economic extinction: the American middle class.

Another byproduct of this multinational globalization centered in America is the creation of a new and previously unseen wave of universal anti-Americanism. We are now viewed as capitalist exploiters of the Third World! If you don't believe me, just ask the foreign-born managers who run one of our sweat shops in the Northern Mariana Islands, the same place my Izod shirt was made a few years ago. Never heard of the place? It's part of the USA out in the Pacific Ocean, and it's where workers and managers are brought from Asia to make clothes very cheaply, then sold for high prices in department stores at home. I don't think I saved any money in the end, just because the shirt was made in a legally established American sweatshop. So in the end, the price to the consumer varies little, but the profits to the companies greatly increases.

American employees' jobs are now also being replaced by foreign workers, who don't even have to set foot in the USA at all in order to do their jobs. With the advent of improved international satellite communications, via computers and telephones, American companies can now establish call centers anywhere they have an English-speaking workhorse. India and the Philippines are now at the forefront of this cheap wave of worker substitutions. People can now work from home all day and just be hooked up to the main call center of their respective company. This cuts down the companies' expenses even further, putting the burden on the employee to provide his own work space, electricity, and supplies. Soon, companies may eventually figure out a way to charge their workers for having a job and make them pay for the privilege of having some sort of employment. We could be heading for the China scenario, where a roof over ones' head and a plate of rice is all we'll get, along with the customary kick in the ass if we get out of line!

AMERICAN FOREIGN RELATIONS

The United States Government, represented by our federal bureaucracy, can only be qualified as a policy of expediency, based upon the economic necessity of that particular administration's political agenda. We must remember, first of all, that politics is the shroud for business and economics in a democracy. In the end, all resolutions of conflicts depend upon the bottom line for those concerned in our country and our client state. All countries are really clients in that they are a market or potential market for American business interests. All of our embassies have a business interests section along with a covert CIA spy operation established everywhere on the globe. Other spy mechanisms are also in place, interwoven inside American businesses abroad. Most wealthy nations work this same way. Our educational institutions funded by government tax dollars also operate abroad and are generally the place of intense covert operations and spying on foreigners and Americans living abroad.

If somebody tried to put a price tag on exactly how much we budget yearly for these practices, we could never actually find out. If one looks at a copy of our Federal Budget, you will never see a line item for CIA operations. It is all magically padded into the budget in other areas, so nobody can ever find out how much we are spending yearly. There is really no accountability anymore, since our military-industrial complex federal government has taken over daily operations. Only a few big wigs in Congress or *The Company*, as it is glibly referred to, may even know.

Taking things such as this in mind, and to further exacerbate the already out-of-control situation, we can also point to the 1.1 Trillion Dollars that go unaccounted for yearly in Defense Department Credit Card fraud. This wanton and wreck-less spending is perpetrated by the very employees of the Department. Nobody ever has any answers, and everybody always promises to put a stop to it, yet the spending never ceases. You now get to bite the bullet in two places, overseas and hometown USA.

HELP MOMS AND HELP THE USA

The foundation of any country's greatness is the family unit, in essence, the backbone of society. All government is based upon the well-being of this ancient and natural organization. Healthy, content, functioning families are capable of helping to create the governmental products of their daily lives. Healthy families are less burdensome overall. A dysfunctional family unit creates additional burdens on society, leading to strains on the government it composes. More costs needed to solve more family problems just makes for higher taxes eventually.

Ever since the American moms have been kicked out of the house to go to work, our society has gone haywire trying to plug the holes in the dikes. By holes I mean divorce, latchkey kids, child neglect, child abuse, and spousal abuse. Kids and moms on drugs are now a common phenomenon, as we see some moms even providing their own children with dope before the school day even begins. They need the calming effects of pot and pills just to make it through their stressful wannabe perfect days.

Rather than trying to plug up the holes, why can't we just do away with the reasons we have for the holes being created in the first place? Maybe if the moms could afford to stay home, even for the afternoon in order to meet and greet their children after school, things might have a chance of improving overall. By taking the tax monies now being spent for hole-plugging and giving it directly to moms, the USA might be able to recapture, at least to some extent, the Ozzie and Harriet-Leave It to Beaver Days of our past. Why not pay moms for staying home to take care of our nation's greatest assets; our children? Raising children and keeping a wholesome home environment takes a lot of hard work, sacrifice, and dedication and deserves at best some consideration for monetary compensation. There are few men interested in the job, so let's clear the path for the maternal instincts by giving people what they really feel they want anyway.

People will call this approach sexist, however, if dads were the ones that wanted to stay home, letting the women work outside the home, then so be it! Many men do great jobs as house husbands and some women prefer to work full time jobs anyway. But the evidence lies with the traditional; moms at home and dads outside the home. Pay the dads or pay the moms, just don't neglect the fragile family unit by throwing the babies out with the bath water.

It is almost certain that we can reduce our government's intervention in the daily lives of the family by reducing the need for its services whenever things go wrong. Courts, police, state and private agencies all now are overwhelmed with matters of the family simply because no one is home watching junior. Moms are so stressed out and just plain burned out from leading a double if not triple life nowadays, its a miracle junior, mom, or dad can muster the energy and courage to get out of bed in the morning. Another upside to this equation will be the lessening of the need for legal and/or illegal drugs to medicate the souls of the stressed-out family members.

We really do not need outsiders telling us how to run our family; what we need is ourselves, so give us back the luxury and give us back our tax money! We may not do it perfectly, but we don't have to anyway. Everyone is entitled to make all the mistakes they want and try to learn from them with their own money. After all, our government makes mistakes everyday anyway and in no way can ever be perfect or better replace family values for its members. "One size fits all families" never works, as each family unit has its own distinct needs or goals. So let's get government out of the homes and give back control to the moms, dads, and children of the USA.

THE DEMISE OF THINKING IN THE USA

Procedures, rules, and regulations have long ago taken the place of common sense, logic, and reason in America. This happened so that corporate government could better control its citizens. Vocational education has gone advanced, working its way from cosmetology, wood shop, home economics, auto repair, and driver education all the way into the graduate schools of our universities. In essence, we continue our education not to find creative ways to improve life, but to learn the ways of fitting the pegs (people) into the holes (corporate America jobs). The time for why or the need for questions has been replaced with pat answers to general situations.

When was the last time you went to a meeting and were not afraid to speak your mind, question hierarchy, or even make any suggestions at work? If you did, you most likely found yourself looking for work very soon afterward. What I am saying is that meetings are a reinforcement of work procedures and not designed to make you work more efficiently to increase profits or cut down on expenses.

Making waves in the civilian world is just like making waves in the military; a sure way to find yourself at a hearing, court-martial, and a nasty discharge. So, next time you feel like collecting unemployment compensation in order to rest for a while, all you have to do is speak up at the next staff meeting, or worse, not even attend.

People have become overly fixated on making money or protecting their precious jobs at any cost; so this means nobody you work with will ever go to bat for you, confide in you, or take any risks for you if it means their economic security may be at stake. American organizations now know this, so they treat people like disposable cups to use our own fear factor as an invisible muzzle and leash to keep us in line as a trained pet might be expected to perform. We need to stop being so scared of the master; we are not their pets. We are creative-spiritual human beings who need full consideration every waking moment of the day. Our American institutions and organizations have to leave room for creative thought, or we shall se smothered by the weight of our own lack of free thought and incompetence.

Our fears, coupled with lack of faith in ourselves to be free cerebrally, will just be the ultimate end of a once great American culture, business world, and society that everyone once wanted to emulate.

GOVERNMENT JOB GLUTTONS

When I first began my quest for a job in Miami in 1972, I found myself at a distinct disadvantage from the get-go. It wasn't the lack of experience that a 22-year-old college graduate had, but the lack of a DD-214 military discharge form. DD stands for Department of Defense, and the 214 shows that someone completed the minimum active duty requirements for military service. Once somebody got this form, they were classified as a veteran by state and federal governments, enabling them to jump to the head of the job line ahead of someone without the same status.

Since I refused to go to Vietnam, became a pacifist, and was honorably discharged from ROTC because of my stance, people always asked me about my lack of the form. I sat there with my long hair and college diploma, trying to explain the situation. Most of the time it didn't play well in Miami, as the USA was still completely controlled by WW2 and Korean War veterans. I had the Honorable Discharge to show, but the fact that I got out of the Army without the required paperwork seemed to irk the system. I suppose it meant that if I hadn't exposed myself to some trumped up enemy, left over from the Cold War, then I wasn't good enough to even work in my own country.

Not only isn't it fair that a religious person be relegated to second banana, but to add insult to injury, someone who actually practices the Ten Commandments (Thou Salt not Kill), is forced to take the scraps left over from those who might have killed another human being. Our American-Global military-industrial complex has even made the task of economic survival that much harder, because of one's personal choices in life. "Nice guys finish last" should be the motto applied to this scenario.

Unfortunately, the benefits to following the leader increase the longer the person allows himself to be a part of the military-industrial complex madness. Somebody who puts in 20 years of military service can get out with a pension for life and still jump to the head of the employment line. This really makes it rough for someone looking for a job, especially a government job. Because state jobs' pay is low and hard for a person to live on, it makes it that much easier for a pensioned person of 40 years of age to accept one. Someone with a state salary and a pension can afford to take the low salary living much more comfortably than, let's say, a 40 year old pacifist with a family, such as myself.

A person who loves America, but in a different manner, has to think very carefully about trying to help his country by taking a civil service job; he just can't afford the luxury of becoming part of the eve-growing legions of the working poor. On the other hand, a guy who gets pensioned off from the Army can become a cop, get another pension from that job, then retire and still work for the city in the Parks and Recreation Department, retiring one more time before he kicks the bucket. The guy hits a triple, while the guy with a conscience barely gets to first base.

Why not level the playing field a little and make life better for Mr. Nice Guy? We can do this by banning people with a government pension from taking another government job. By freeing up the jobs for the other kind of Americans, we might actually be able to change the face of our government enough to make a real difference in the future. Religious people, who actually practice what they preach, might be able to make the USA a kinder, gentler place for everyone. We could get people in government who actually will turn our spears into pruning hooks and our chariots into plows. We need people in government who will put our tax dollars to work at home again and for our own citizens.

War veterans are nice to have as long as they have actually defended our country from a real enemy. They are needed in government to remind us of the stupidity and horrors of war. But a cross-section of varied citizens running our country is essential to our long term economic survival and domestic well-being. We simply can't go on forever looking for or creating wars to artificially stimulate our economy. The fake sugar economic high only wears off, making America feel worn out and too tired to face the future with energy and resolution.

LET'S LEGALIZE AND REGULATE OUR CRIME

In our country, alcohol use is taken for granted by most members of our society. It is allowed to be advertised on television and in the print media as well. However, it used to be against the law in the entire country, under Constitutional Law. Religious people at the turn of the 20th Century realized how bad it was for everyone overall and banned it. But as we know, that strategy backfired and just created an underground economy run by organized crime. As long as people want something badly enough, it can be provided at a cost, no matter the consequences.

Now alcohol consumption is an interwoven socially acceptable part of everyday life. It is highly regulated by the government and taxed under the "sin tax" category along with tobacco and gambling. Meyer Lansky predicted that the state would get involved in the business of gambling once they realized how much money they could make themselves; hence the state lottery systems mushroomed.

The legal drug companies are also highly regulated by the FDA. Many of their products are highly addictive, and yet are socially acceptable, like alcohol and tobacco. Some of the legal drugs kill or maim the public; law suits ensue and maybe the drugs are later taken off the market to avoid further problems. Yet the same giant multinational drug companies continue to do business as usual, while none of their owners or leaders goes to prison. However, the illegal pusher-man does not have the same social net to protect him from his customers getting sick or dying from a bad dose of the wrong stuff. The pusher-man goes straight to jail and does not pass Go.

Our country has what we could call an over-reliance upon chemical medicines that, of course, are all very legal. They may hurt or kill you, but at least the doctor gave it to you with a prescription. We are just beginning to try and break those chemically imposed bonds, reverting to more natural ways of treating illnesses. Healthy alternatives are showing that the legalized chemicals being dumped into our bodies can be stopped. Homeopathy is making a comeback in our country and many health issues once reserved for the MD pill-pushers are now being looked at differently as alternative medicine is getting a chance. Vitamins, herbs, aromatherapy, acupuncture, and massage are examples of how we are beginning to look at health matters differently.

If these kinds of alternatives are now tolerated, then perhaps we should look at the alternative to the failed war on drugs, just another made-up war to help grow our government to its mammoth size. Remember, when the government doesn't actually have a real war to fight, it creates one to keep feeding the military-industrial complex and the new police state order we supposedly need to protect us (from ourselves). The idea of citizen security can be and is being used to control people, thereby giving us fewer rights in our ever-weakening democracy.

The alternative is to legalize drugs, with strict medical supervision for addicts. An addict should not have to beg, borrow, and steal to feed his habit. With a medical prescription, people can lead a normal life, possibly even getting off them with time and counseling. Right now, only a very wealthy person can afford proper rehabilitation to wean him off of drugs like cocaine or heroin. Assuming we can tax the new legal drugs, then the money could be used for education and treatment centers to try and keep others off the same dreadful path that dooms them to addiction. Right now, organized crime is in a worldwide war with governments to eradicate coca and poppy fields. Armed conflict all related to the international drug trade causes death and destruction daily. By taking the big money away from the players through legalization, it is bound to put a huge dent in the military-industrial's daily war games and the crooks' incentives to continue being criminals.

Once we can put away the machine guns and helicopters, stop the soldiers and bad guys from killing each other for nothing, and come to our collective senses, a kinder, more gentle approach will be implemented toward the sick people hooked on drugs. The new approach can also give job opportunities to good, honest, hardworking people who are against the idea of killing for a living. Educated, caring, religious, and sensitive people with good minds could replace the crooks, cops, and soldiers now making the headlines daily. They could work as program managers or treatment counselors in the new centers that will be set up by the taxes collected on the cocaine and heroin sales. Then TV shows will not just feature an assortment of super cops, soldiers, and bad guys, but nice guys who don't like to carry guns or kill people. Our police state mentality will be eroded as well and freedom will raise its head once again.

A lot less people will be put behind bars once the drug legalization programs begins. A lot of money can be saved just from the prison explosion being capped and reduced once the new laws and programs begin to take effect. Many people in prison are addicts and dealers. As soon as many of them get out now, they hit the streets once again and wind up back in the slammer. Drug legalization, control, taxing, and treatment will stop the revolving prison door, thereby cutting down on policing and prison costs. This could also free up tax monies for education in schools or be used to make free and low cost community-based clinics for the poor and indigent. If Americans just learned to face up to the error of their ways with regard to the constant fabrication of wars, all Americans could be assured a much higher quality of life, with a strong national health care system in place for the needy.

ORGANIZED CRIME;
TOLERATED OR NOT?

As a native Miamian, I always wondered what it would be like to be a member of organized crime, kind of like the people living in my area of the planet. After all, Al Capone used to live on Palm Island, and I used to pass by his old mansion many times on my way to Miami Beach. He used to stay at the Biltmore Hotel in Coral Gables, a highly respected establishment of our proper society. He also helped to organize the Westview Country Club, where golf is still being played there today. His insistence on constructing a high watchtower at the facility enabled him and the boys to spot the cops before they got too close to the place.

Meyer Lansky, another household name, eventually moved down to Miami Beach and lived in a beautiful beachfront condo on Collins Avenue, not too far from the Fontainebleau Hotel. He was a New Yorker and founder of Murder Incorporated that made money doing hits for anybody that needed his services. Sometimes when I used to eat at a popular deli near his home on 41st street on the Beach, I'd glance at some framed photos of him hanging on the wall near the booth where I used to sit. He was an icon, a celebrity that people quietly worshiped from afar. He was the kind of guy you wished you could be like, but dare not tell anyone!

Most of the gangsters were either Catholic like Al Capone or Jewish like Meyer Lansky. They remained Kosher or Legit, by socializing with the society patrons and matrons in their area. They gave large donations to the right charities or even began their own soup kitchens as Al Capone did in Chicago. Rabbis, priests, and bishops would never say "no" to their generosity; allowing these type of citizens to fit in and walk freely among the community.

These gangsters are mentioned to show an example of how our society tolerated and continues to allow certain types of criminal activity as long as it doesn't get too loud, messy, and obvious to the community. What we need to do is completely disassociate ourselves from this element of our society once and for all, look at ourselves in the mirror, and say "no" to the easy money they can provide for us as a civilized community. Our possible fantasies of mob life should never come in to erase our integrity or our dignity, which is grounded in honesty and morality. Just remember that this sort of attitude not only should apply to gangster mentality, but to government and corporate greed and corruption, the most widespread and socially acceptable kind we have in the world today.

Our nation can only remain strong and free as long as its citizens undertake their role in a democratic society, speaking out by denouncing such examples of corruption and evil. Every citizen has the duty and the right to pressure their representatives to answer to them when the need arises and vote for the kind of leaders they can really trust with the lives of their families.

CRUMBLING SCHOOLS-
CRUMBLING SOCIETY

While fresh on the topic of gangsterism and corruption, why not explore the shadowy world of the American public school systems?. This has become one of the biggest businesses and employers in America today. It employs all strata of society under one roof, basically at the same time. At the bottom of the food chain are the custodial staff, bus drivers, crossing guards, cafeteria workers, and clerks. The teachers and other instructional staff are somewhere in the middle. Administrative staff such as principals, specialists, and area office directors is creeping toward the top of the pyramid. However, the big players, where the heavy money is made, are the contractors, lobbyists, superintendents, school board members, and the politically connected insiders.

Everyday, millions of dollars are wasted or just plain stolen by relatives and cronies inside the school systems. Slow or sloppy construction of schools, combined with decrepit and unsafe classrooms, make Johnny unable to read or socially function at an acceptable level. Schools have become a babysitting service for the young and a daily detention center for the teenage students. People are being forced to attend school until they are 16 years of age, but the instability of the environment being offered does not allow them to succeed very well.

School systems always promise to change or improve, but the changes always take too long to implement. Teachers are under so much stress and pressure to conform to standards; that they can't really do much actual teaching anymore. The politicians, mostly men with law degrees, have universally used the classroom teachers as whipping boys or scapegoats for their failure to supply quality to our nation's student population. It is extremely easy to pick on a teacher, but just try to teach in a classroom for one day and you find out exactly how tough it is. Meanwhile, bad contractors keep getting new and fatter contracts while teachers unions are in bed with management to protect the status quo of underpaid and overworked teachers.

Some years ago, there was a slogan saying that "Johnny can't read!" But today's new mantra has to be that "Johnny doesn't want to read." Johnny simply is not interested anymore at all, as the audio-visual world of computers, TV. and I-pods take over the minds of the young. Students get turned off to the whole educational process because they are nothing but robots used to fill test level quotas. Those mandates were implemented by meddling politicians, who made their political mark by attacking teachers in the first place. If all our society cares about is artificial scores rattled out by computer analysis, this is the way. But if we really want well-educated students, we must clean up the political corruption and meddling by outsiders; that means non-educators such as career politicians.

The first place to save money for schools is to get rid of school principals and let the schools be run by teachers alone. Teachers can rotate being the head teacher of the school by democratic vote, thus giving everyone a real chance to make changes for their school. Instead of ignoring teachers with 30 years of experience at the same school, give people like this the opportunity to sail the boat once in a blue moon. It is these kinds of people who really know the community the best, not some temporary administrator from downtown, on a mission to fatten his pay check until he can retire with a fat pension.

When a person can teach well, likes to teach, and really cares about the quality of the learning environment, it behooves schools to retain these people at a salary that merits their contribution. Teacher salaries are low, because presently the school systems have absolutely no intention to keep them for more than 5 years. That is why teachers' unions know only too well to base their dues on the beginning teacher's salary. Unions negotiate this end of the salary range as much as they can and deliberately neglect the legions of loyal teachers who stick with the program for extended periods of time. This way it is easy to attract new conscripts but then becomes very difficult to retain them, once they get frustrated and burned out! School systems and unions know the scenario and appear to be in an unspoken collusion to keep everything the same. In the end, school systems get teachers on the cheap because they don't stay long. Teachers' unions keep getting more and more dues money as the beginning teacher's salary goes up more than the other steps on the salary ladder.

It is a miracle that Johnny can read at all, considering the corrupt business deals, the political meddling, the nepotistic bureaucracies, labor—management collusion, crumbling facilities, outdated materials, lack of supplies, overworked teachers, and, most important of all, the lack of parental concern or responsibility for their children. Parents look at schools as a 24/7 baby sitting service, complete with at least two nutritious meals a day. Public schools are a place for learning and for those actually interested in the process. If a student is not on the same page as the teachers that is only because their home life mimics their disinterest.

Parents and caretakers must focus on this importance to become an educated person and instill high levels of it in the entire process from the time their child is in pre-school. Failure to do so will make it absolutely impossible for any student to achieve much academically, socially, and possibly economically in the future.

Since the United States has compulsory education until the age of 16, we take it all for granted, along with the free ride. However, if parents were pressured to exert influence on their children, their lethargic attitudes might change. If they were told they could no longer get a free education or they had to find a school that would accept them, Johnny might buckle down and start to study in order to pass his classes. The possible threat that implies that a child must either shape up or ship out could very well get the irresponsible parent's attention long enough to make a difference. But if there is no parents at home or just one parent, this process becomes increasingly difficult to get Johnny to pay attention and study. Current statistics show that 25% of white children, 50% of Hispanic children, and 70% of black children are born out of wedlock today. If people are reproducing with absolutely no consideration of the underlying consequences, the societal infrastructure severely weakens. No country can be successful educating its children if nobody is home minding the kids, nurturing them, giving them values, and making sure of the details needed to properly raise a child.

MODERN WARS DON'T REVIVE AILING ECONOMIES

War is the best business in the world and also the best way to control people. War is a sugar high for a country's economy. It temporarily helps infuse money into the system, but soon turns ugly when the treasury has to borrow money to continue financing its onward march in a culture of death. But since the take over of America by our military-industrial complex culture, the United States needs to keep finding new and improved places and reasons to keep us on a war footing.

All the tax money diverted to military madness is money not being spent on health care, education, the arts and sciences, local infrastructures, national security, children, the elderly, family counseling, drug or alcohol rehabilitation, and diplomacy. In the end, military—industrial complex cultures benefit the few at the expense of the many. It perpetuates a permanent hierarchy of power based upon corruption; it destroys the morality of our social fabric, ultimately destroying the very strength upon which the whole leadership was based. "Those who live by the sword shall perish by the sword." (Matthew 26:52.). How much longer can we continue to live on the edge of destruction? Either we will implode from within through greed and corruption, or we will be wiped out by our present and future enemies, more numerous and powerful together than the 300 million of us.

Let's take our blood money and get the military-industrialists to help us by developing our infrastructure, cure our social ills, and get us to reach our perfect potential of greatness with freedom and dignity. These humble adjustments to our conformist and death-oriented culture, I will assure us our place as the world leader from now until eternity. To disregard our present path of folly will only hasten our own demise, actually helping our enemies to push us down further in defeat and humiliation.

All this is easier said than done, so it is going to take everyone interested in our harmonious survival to change their way of thinking. We must shout in unison to get our national, state, and local leaders to see the light, smell the coffee, and wake up before it is too late to do anything about it. Everyone should participate more in the democratic process by at least voting in every election in which they are asked. About half of us don't ever vote in anything or are registered. Democracy can only survive if we actively participate by overseeing our elected and non-elected masters. But to make real and permanent change, Americans have to reform the election system nationwide. It needs to be made more democratic and inclusive to all sectors of society, not just an amusement park for those who can pay to enter and go on the rides.

REFORM THE ELECTION SYSTEM

✦

(Parts here are previously covered in other sections)

The best way to change the direction of America is to disallow all PAC, or political action committees. These PACs are nothing more than a strainer to give bribe money to politicians, so it appears that everything in Washington and our state capitols is kosher. Supposedly, bribery is illegal in our country, but not the giving of money to organizations for political, social, religious, or economic reasons.

The United States has to be by far the most over-organized organization of organizations ever concocted by mankind. If you have a cause or a gripe, you can find a group that is very well organized to take your money. However, that does not mean that your money will be spent to actually help you with your problem. Most likely, what will happen is that you will be made a lot of empty promises, and the people running the group will fatten their bank accounts. They may actually have to do a bit of what they promise, but that is usually done only to allow them to continue their organization's existence. Organizations' methods are like police departments; they catch 10% of the criminals, and then advertise the deed while turning a blind eye to the rest of them. The question "Where's a cop when you need one?" has to come from something based on experience.

If you are not one of the organization's own, you don't have a snowball's chance in hell to get their attention without flashing the cash. That goes double for politicians! If you want to talk to the president, it will cost you at least $25,000 and up to bend his ear. Crooks have been known to have even been pardoned by American presidents in the past. Of course, the pardon came after the deed and the person were first legally sanitized in anticipation of taking the cash, I mean pardon!

Another way to stop the corruption and demise of democracy in America is to not even allow direct campaign contributions to politicians in any form, including small public ones of $25. Politicians need to get a good salary if they work for us, and that is it. If they do a bad job, then they should be voted out of office quickly by their constituents.

So, how do politicians and public office seekers get the money to campaign, you ask? That is easy! Take a fraction of the newly found available tax money, being diverted from our war machines and use that to pay for their expenses. Everybody running for office will get exactly the same amount of taxpayer based funds, thereby completely leveling the political playing field in each election. Why should some obsequious, corrupt, self-serving lackey for a big military-industrialist-related complex company always win the election? Well, he shouldn't! The retired teacher or stay at home mom should; that is, if she's got what it takes to do the job! But as of today's reading of this book, her chances of winning are slim to none! We all know that it is political suicide for our leaders to enact new legislation overhauling American politics and government, but we can start someplace and the time is now! Remember that the truth shall set you free, because right now you are probably a slave of the lies and deception that make the few fat cats your masters. Remember, you've got the power in your hands to make the change, and your leaders know it! We need to get honest, new blood in leadership positions and then limit their terms in all capacities, whether it is local, state, or national levels of politics.

Right now the Democrat and Republican parties are playing a never-ending game of ping pong with your balls. They control the table, the rackets, the net, and the rules of play. However, they take it for granted that nobody else wants to play or even use their own taxpayer-paid for equipment. Right now, if another political party wants to grab a racket and participate in the game, the two major parties will hog the table until you decide to just go away. If you try to take a racket while they are playing, without their permission, then you will wind up in jail for trying to overthrow the government (actually the republicrats). The two major political parties just take turns serving and winning the games. A political party always needs a convenient opponent to attack and vilify in order to get your money and perpetuation. So it is in their vested interest to keep hogging the table to keep you and me out of their private game. If they can continue getting our money and votes, there is no reason to give up their winning strategy.

COPY CAT NEWS
DISTRACTIONS

How many times have you turned on the TV news, began surfing the channels, and noticed that everybody was covering the same stories at the same time? More likely, it happened more times than you could count. Did you ever wonder why the major news services all report on more or less the same things on a regular basis? It doesn't make sense for this to occur, as news services and TV networks are supposedly competing for your viewing time. However, this is exactly what is happening in America today.

Radio news basically does the same thing as TV news, in that all of the coverage you hear is about the same. It's actually very hard to find alternative news sources on mainstream TV or radio broadcasts.

Let's start with the notion that each major network works independently of its rival; then how could it be possible that at the end of the day, everybody winds up covering almost all the same news stories? Do the news bureau chiefs call each other and have a pow wow to figure out what their stations will air that day? Maybe there is a news ombudsman that advises everybody what should go on the radio and TV. Perhaps there exists an independent council of news moms and dads whose sole job is to give the thumbs up or down on news stories. I don't think so, but it does make you wonder about how this could happen on a daily basis.

The reason might just be that in the news business, the corporate culture likes to report on stories that are friendly to their way of doing things. They look for stories that are not going to be a threat to their world business model or the American government's day-to-day methods of running the country. It is no surprise, then, that corporations ruling the planet, such as General Electric, have bought control of news services like NBC. What chance could there be for fair and accurate reporting of events that might be detrimental to a large company's bottom line? The answer is none. So, if the hard hitting stories that deeply question the status quo or conventional wisdom are eliminated, then in the end there must only be a few stories that have enough appeal to even make it to the viewing screen. Those safe stories, combined with fluff news, pieces are what are being presented to the American viewing public on a daily basis.

It is almost as if there was a conscious effort to keep us from knowing what is really going on in the world, an effort to subtly brainwash us and lull us into a sense of contentment. TV is a very powerful tool that has been proven to allow government-corporate alliances to pacify and convert viewers into agreeable and loyal citizens. After all, what better way could there be to get everybody on the same page or wavelength than by periodic doses of purified news programming? This wouldn't be the first time something like this has happened to people.

The Nazis figured this out and were years ahead of the USA in using the media to control its citizenry. Their organization of gangsters even had a Ministry of Propaganda, run by Dr. Goebbels to turn the average German citizen into a hate machine, capable of killing innocent people deemed non-Aryan. But, don't feel bad; we are not alone in this kind of persuasive information business. Every country basically does the same thing to unify its people, in the direction their leaders want them to go. People desire security above all, and the collective consciousness of the group mentality makes people feel better, when they think they belong to the same wonderful group In the end, nobody wants to feel like an oddball or the square peg in the round hole.

All this non-conventional wisdom might lead us to believe that in the end there is no such thing as a truly free press. Even the press has its limitations, yet perhaps it doesn't want to recognize them right now. Our country does have more freedoms than in other countries, but since there is no such thing as a perfect world, there is always room for more improvement. Our American press needs to take more chances exposing lies, corruption, deception, and all the other dirty little secrets in government that never see the light of day. Journalists have to push their readers to constantly question the mandated authority their government has been given and sacredly entrusted. To do any less would be a clear signal for our leaders to take us for granted even more than they do now.

Average Americans are the salvation of their nation, not outsiders, pundits, paid lobbyists, politicians and the like. A hard working family knows what it needs to succeed on a day-to-day basis, and their instincts are what lead them. We Americans can smell a rat a mile away; the problem is that we are so badly distracted most of the time by external influences that we can't make our wishes and desires known for implementing change. The news dribble, the commercials, the rush of our busy lives, and the daily needs of survival do not give us the time needed to shout out from the rafters to demand the respect our leaders have long ago forgotten.

WHAT'S THE REMEDY?

If you want to get respect and change, try some of these or all on a regular basis:

1. Vote in every election. Local elections really count the most in the end, as they influence national trends. Don't just vote for the President once every four years.

2. Write e-mail and/or letters to all of your political leaders; that includes judges!

3. Make appointments to personally visit your leaders so they know you are out there and mean business! The squeaky wheel gets the grease.

4. Join and participate in groups that matter to you for implementing change, as there is strength in numbers. Get your own website going this way!

5. Speak your mind on matters of concern to your friends and neighbors every time you get the chance. A pebble tossed in the lake makes ripples and makes changes.

6. Do not, under any circumstances, underestimate yourself and your ability to influence others. Your commitment and passion will carry you over the rough spots when you may get to the point, when you begin to think that nobody is listening to you!

7. Contact the media, especially radio and print, in order to make them aware of your concerns. This should be used as one of your last resorts after you've already tried one of the above techniques. Build your case of rejection first to catch the bums with their pants down!

8. Get permits to stage a street protest, even if it's just you carrying a home-made sign in front of the school board office; you've got the right under the constitution. (Refer to #7)

9. Write a protest song, poem, book, play, or screenplay to get attention, and try to market it to get the attention it deserves. The pen is mightier than the sword. (Refer to #7)

10. Control your temper and emotions, never resorting to violence in any form. The strongest changes come from non-violent protest. The system is set up to keep you from changing it, and the massive, amount of laws make it very easy for you to get tripped up, if you fall into the violence trap that's been set for you.

11. Never break the law, unless you actually want to go to jail as a symbolic protest! Jail really sucks, if you know what I mean. But if you do break the law by accident, then be ready for spending quality time with Big Bubba or Big Momma!

12. If things get really rough, do not forget that God is always with you, to pick you up when you are down. Prayer really helps a lot, so keep a Bible handy.

THE FAT LADY SINGS HER SONG

While I was in the process of writing this book, I happened to mention it to an English acquaintance of mine in passing. I explained to him that the book consisted of an analysis of the good and the bad of the United States. With his razor-sharp British wit, he quickly stated that the book would have a few pages on the good, followed by massive amounts of pages on the bad aspects of American life. He turned out to be right. However as a reader, don't think that the bad outweighs the good simply because more pages are devoted to constructive criticism. The great things that make my country so wonderful all speak for themselves, but we just need to be reminded of them sometimes. It's the negative parts of American life which we are constantly reminded of daily.

In order for us to move ahead as a people with the desire to form a more perfect union, we have to keep trying to improve upon what we have without destroying all the great aspects of American life and society. This takes time, complicated analysis and soul searching. If we just accept the fact that we need this from time to time, then we are all going to be better off in the end. We all have the responsibility to help our nation keep its leadership position in the world, not slip back by resting on its laurels. A democracy is a fragile concoction which takes lots of grooming to keep in proper shape. All aspects of a nation's structure constantly need inspection and minor changes when deemed necessary.

Ask yourself this question: do you want Ray Bradbury's vision of the future seen in <u>Fahrenheit 451?</u> This is a futuristic world in which books are banned and burned; kids amuse themselves with random violence; dumbed-down people escape on pills, getting lost in a world of interactive TV on big, wall-sized screens. If "no way" Jose is your answer, get moving in a new direction; some place you've never ventured before. Get active, get vocal, get the lead out, and hold your leaders accountable for their actions before you can't even vote for them anymore. If you don't want to be herded like cattle anymore, you won't be, as long as you break free and participate in your wonderfully resilient democratic nation; the

Greatest Country in the World! Remember; if you don't use it, you lose it! DEMOCRACY! FREEDOM! HAPPINESS! PEACE! WEALTH!

If I were the Fat Lady at the end of an opera, singing away, then I guess that this would make this the end of the book. But I want to end with the hope that soon we can seriously take stock of ourselves to find the best way possible for all Americans to truly say that their country really is the best place in the world to live. Nobody needs to be without food, a home, or medical attention in such a nation of plenty. Everybody's needs, desires, wishes, hopes, and dreams can become reality with some old-fashioned values exerted by all of us!

I'll never forget the old Superman program from the 1950's. It stated that Superman stood for truth, justice, and the American way. So let's be Superman in our own way. Let's fight for the way things ought to be and take away the chance for people with a criminal mentality to further ruin the goodness we have left as a nation. The golden rule states to do unto others as you would have them do unto you. It is not, "He who has the gold makes the rules!" We all need to live fairly amongst each other. The keepers of the gold do not deserve to be treated better by being allowed to make the rules in favor of themselves any longer. Our future as a viable democracy demands this. Once this sinks in, then and only then can we go to sleep at night, assured that when we awaken, our rights as free men and women will still be there! With this in mind, remember: Nobody's Perfect!

978-0-595-42084-1
0-595-42084-2

Made in the USA
Monee, IL
14 June 2020